# Reflections

*Looking at Timeless Truths
In a Changing World*

*John Lancaster*

*Copyright © John Lancaster 2010*

Contact:

Cover design by Graham Alder

ISBN 978-0-9561996-7-6

# Life Publications

# Foreword

**M**uch of the contents of this book appeared originally under the title "And Finally…" in *Direction,* the monthly magazine published by the Elim Pentecostal Church. The constraints of writing 600 or so words for the back page of the magazine meant that the treatment of any subject could not be in depth. For that reason, the title *Reflections* has been chosen, but as the sub-title suggests, the articles are still a serious attempt to suggest lines of thought on matters which are spiritually and practically important in today's changing world.

Busy modern people seem not to have the time or inclination to plough through books or even read long chapters, regrettable though that may be, so it was felt that these short articles on a wide spectrum of themes could give such busy people the opportunity of taking a fresh look, from slightly different angles, at "time-less truths" in the hope that it would provoke new avenues of thought on some of the things we tend to take for granted. We have attempted to arrange the wide range of subjects in a simple framework which will allow the reader to "dip" here and there in a profitable way. These are "snacks" rather than "three-course meals", but they may perhaps keep some travellers sustained on their journey and whet their appetites for something more substantial.

These "reflections" are the musings of a pastor who has tried over many years to keep in touch with the ever-changing patterns of life and ministry in the contemporary world while seeking to "understand the times" from a biblical perspective. It is his hope that they do genuinely catch the light of the Word and the Spirit. He wishes to thank John Glass, the General Superintendent of the Elim Pentecostal Church, for permission to reprint the articles from *Direction* and Peter Wreford at New Life Publishing Co. for his help in making them available. And finally, his sincere thanks to David and Jan Holdaway for the encouragement and tremendous help they have given in preparing the book for publication.

*John Lancaster*

# Reflections

# Encountering God

# *Reflections*

## *Meeting God in the Courts of the Morning*

The house stood amidst trees set back from the road. It was large and imposing, standing on an escarpment overlooking a beautiful valley which, with its clusters of trees, wide meadows and winding streams, stretched as far as the eye could see. To quote the psalmist, it was *"beautiful for situation"*. To me, who as a teenager passed it quite frequently, its name was as beautiful as its situation. It was called "The Courts of the Morning". I imagined sitting on the verandah with friends and family in the calm of early morning, watching the sun rise over distant hills, listening to the sweet sound of the dawn chorus, and breathing in the freshness of an unspoiled day. With the sun flooding the valley and the broad terraces of the house with golden light and welcome warmth, it seemed the epitome of peace and beauty.

The teenager whose imagination was thus inspired never did watch the sunrise from "The Courts of the Morning"; he never had an invitation to breakfast! To the privileged inhabitants of that secluded house he was an anonymous outsider. But he was not unduly troubled, because he, too, was privileged. Along with millions of other ordinary people he could sing, *"Blessed are those you choose and bring near to live in your courts!"*(Psalm 65:4). He knew what it was to stand in spirit with the psalmist – and sparrows and swallows – in the courts of the Lord (Psalm 84:1-4,10) and to watch with Malachi (4:2) the *"sun of righteousness...rise with healing in its wings"*.

Entry into the courts of the Lord demands clean hands and a pure heart (Psalm 24:3-6), and a worshipping spirit (Psalm 96:8; 100:2-4). It is a holy place into which only those who have humbly sought cleansing from sin may come. But it is also a place of abundant grace (Psalm 36:8), stimulating companionship (Psalm 116:18,19), and spectacular views, for there *"your eyes will see the king in his beauty and view a land that stretches afar"* (Isaiah 33:17).

Today, from my study window I watched the sunrise – not over purple hills and a lush green valley but from behind the roof of a local supermarket and an inner-city rugby ground! But it was still stunning. The glory of gilt-edged clouds back-lit by the morning sun was just as great here as it would have been over those lovely Hampshire meadows. Location cannot prevent the sunrise. By the same token, whoever we are and whatever our circumstances, access to the "Courts of the Morning" is always open to those who will make time to *"ascend the hill of the Lord and stand in his holy place"*. With an open Bible and a heart likewise open to the Spirit, fellowship with God in *"the secret place of the Most High"* promises rich rewards.

For instance, join Habakkuk, the questioning prophet, as he discusses the contemporary world situation with God (Habakkuk 1), climb up to his watch tower (2:1f.) as he listens to what God has to say. Reverently bow your head as he pours out his heart in passionate prayer (3:1, 2), then share his gasp of astonishment as the awesome glory of the holiness and power of God storm across a shuddering political landscape like a tsunami of judgment (3:3-16). Here in the "courts of the Lord" we are privileged to stand at the nerve-centre of the universe, at the hub of history, and the place where the destiny of the world is decided. Yet here, Habakkuk whispers (3:17-19), is also the place where a trembling human being can find security and peace – a place where the awesome Lord of the universe stoops down tenderly and ministers like a divine "chiropodist" to enable his servant to negotiate the challenging mountain heights with the agility of a deer. Habakkuk's prayer (3:2) is answered – in wrath God does *"remember mercy"*.

What a view there is from this place! It really is worth the climb to "The Courts of the Morning".

## *Making Room for God*

**A** girl was sitting at her school desk in an old fashioned Scripture lesson, so the story goes, when she raised her hand and asked, "Is God everywhere, Miss?" Receiving a positive answer, she probed a little deeper, "Is he in this classroom, Miss?"

Aware she was treading on dangerous ground, the teacher nodded hesitantly. Then came the crunch question. Pointing to the inkwell in her desk the youthful theologian asked, "Is he in my inkwell, Miss?"

Explaining immanence to an eight-year-old is not easy, so the teacher murmured less confidently, "Erm...well...yes, I suppose in a way he is."

A moment later the brooding silence was broken by the sound of the little girl clapping her hand over the inkwell and triumphantly exclaiming, "Got him!"

You may think that story somewhat far-fetched, or even a bit irreverent, but the truth is that nearly all of us, in some way or another, try to contain God within the confines of our own "inkwells" of theology, church structures and personal preferences.

We do it in our theology because we so often come to the Bible and read it through the lenses of our particular make of religious spectacles. We read it – and frequently read "into" it things we call "insights" – but the trouble is that our spectacles are often "bifocal". They tend to blur the distinction between what the Word actually says and what our particular spiritual background says it says. Some neat doctrinal outlines gleaned from here and there, and a collection of convenient proof texts, and we feel we've "got him", though we wouldn't put it quite like that. The truth is, our theological inkwells are too shallow. Listen to Job's friend, Zophar (Job 13:7 and 8): *"Can you fathom the mysteries of God? Can you probe the limits of the Almighty? They are higher than the heavens – what can you do? They are deeper than the depths of the grave – what can you know?"*

Better still, listen to Paul's outbreak of ecstatic praise in Romans 11:33f: *"O the depth of the riches of the wisdom and knowledge of God! How unsearchable his judgements and his ways beyond tracing out!"*

Thank God for all that he has revealed to us, for the great certainties on which faith rests and about which we can be uncompromising. But the well of truth is deeper than our tiny "inkwells" and we do well to humble ourselves before him. We don't know it all!

The "inkwell" mentality of a people dreaming dreams of future glory was challenged through God's Word in Isaiah's day (Isaiah 66:1-6). God said, *"Your ecclesiastical structures* (verse one) *and your religious practices* (verse three) *can never contain the reality of my holy, all-pervading presence."*

Yet so often we seem to believe that that certain models of church structure and certain methods of ministry and certain forms of worship will guarantee the presence and blessing of God. We go to conferences, attend seminars, read books, watch videos, log onto websites, and visit so-called "successful" churches – in the hope of finding the elusive secret. But often it is all "inkwell" stuff! We are trying to capture within man-made parameters what God has assigned to the freedom of the Spirit. As the New Testament by its silence on the matter clearly reveals, there is no final definitive model of church structure or "order" of ministry. Principles, yes; explicit blueprint, no.

What God really desires is not architectural splendours, impressive organisational structures, beautiful liturgies, or the latest so-called "cutting edge" styles of ministry and worship. Rather, he's looking for "humble" and "contrite" men and women – aware of their total inadequacy and dependency upon him – who "tremble" and respond reverently and willingly to his Word (verse two). They're the people God keeps his eye on. Out of them, not out of the "inkwells" of human self-confidence, will flow rivers of living water.

## *The Potentate of Time*

One of the few benefits of the wartime blackout was the fact that with all the street lights off, you could actually see the stars.

It is a strange reflection on the fallenness of man that in the illumination of his towns and cities he has created what has become known as "light pollution". The haze created by ill-designed lighting and the fumes of industry and traffic has obscured the skies – a parable in itself. Pollution with rubbish is at least understandable, but pollution with light? Only sinners could achieve that.

My memories of the blackout in southern England are still vivid. I remember the long white fingers of searchlights probing the sky and ruffling the clouds as they searched for the German bombers high above the South Downs. We knew they were Heinkels because of the tell-tale throb-throb drone of their engines. Every now and then we saw them trapped like giant moths in a brilliant web of concentrated light, and to a fourteen year-old not yet aware of the bloody realities of war, there was a certain excitement in it all. But for that same fourteen year-old the blackout held another fascination. To sit by an open window and gaze up at the brilliance of the stars amid the deep silences of the surrounding countryside was to enter a world of mysterious and awe-inspiring dimensions. The vastness of it, the glory of it – like diamonds, he thought, scattered across a huge cloth of black velvet – and the permanence of it, save for the occasional bright fall of a shooting star, brought to him an awareness that somewhere beyond the ordinary routine of his life – home, school, play, Saturday job, and Sundays at church – and beyond the droning Heinkel bombers and the still distant war and rumours of war, there was a world – or worlds – of overwhelming vastness and indescribable wonder.

But there was more. From his open window as the night wind whispered through the trees at the bottom of the garden he caught glimpses of eternity. How did it all begin? In his simple way he knew the answer to that – *"In the beginning God created the heaven and earth..."* But what of before *"the beginning"*? What was it like to be "eternal" – to have no beginning, to go back, and back, and back, and back and still have no starting point? Or for that matter, to go on, and on, and on, and on...for ever and ever and ever. Such thoughts filled him with a certain dread. Sometimes he wasn't sure whether he wanted to "have everlasting life". It seemed too much to take in. Life as he knew it, with its succession of days and weeks, birthdays and Christmas, was at least measurable, even if painfully slow at times, but eternity seemed like time out of control, an unknown quantity that filled him at times with nameless awe... and all the while the stars looked down, unwavering and unanswerable in their brilliance.

His "intimations of immortality" were vague but they still provided a misty horizon to his life; he knew within him that the Bible could be trusted when it spoke of God the Creator and Lord of life. There had been the day when, gently led by his older brother, he had received the Lord Jesus Christ as his personal Saviour. Out of that encounter and an ongoing, if sometimes wavering, fellowship with Jesus and in His Word, and the faithful care of fellow Christians, he had learned at least something of what it meant to be a believer. There was much he didn't know, and much he just didn't understand, but in a simple way he could say, *"I know whom I have believed and am persuaded that He is able to keep that which is committed unto Him against that day..."* But eternity! That was different – too difficult to grasp.

Had he known it, in his simple way he had joined the greatest philosophers who had ever lived, was one with Aristotle, Plato, Hegel, and a host of other brilliant minds who toyed with notions of eternity and got lost in dense jungles of speculative thought. And as he grew older and his horizons grew wider he learned that contemporary thinkers are still lost – and some of them like the author of *A Brief History of Time*, are extremely impatient, sometimes arrogantly so, because their latest theories are only philosophical buckets riddled with "black holes" which cannot even hold the water of time, let alone the oceans of eternity.

Yet, deny it or dread it, the sense of "something beyond us" still breaks into the closed-circuits of our self absorption, because it is God-given – *"He has also set eternity in the hearts of men"* (Ecclesiastes 3:11).

It is not only philosophers who have a sense of lostness. Ordinary people feel it too, as a letter from a boyhood friend whom I had not seen for 50 years reminded me just recently. It recounted his life over those years, its highs and lows, joys and sorrows. Great achievements rubbed shoulders with broken marriages; sudden and tragic death walked hand in hand with dreams fulfilled. All in all it was a typical story of human life as most people live it. Then came the explosion, "I am convinced that man has made God in his own image because his colossal deceit would not allow him to believe that, when life is extinct that is the end. He has become the planet's most dangerous predator and will eventually bring about his own extinction along with many other life forms. So eat, drink, and be merry, for tomorrow we die!"

I remembered him back in the days when he came to church with me – a fair haired boy who shared the fun of youthful innocence. Now, it seemed, the harsh realities of life had burned that early faith down to the cold ash of pessimism.

Against the background of a world in which evil seems to hold sway, where injustice and man's inhumanity to man inflict unbearable wounds and where greed, lying and selfishness have turned the world into a moral desert, it is not surprising that men find it hard to believe. "Where is God in all this?" is not always a cynical reaction; it is often the cry of genuinely lost people, the groan of deep despair.

But there is an answer to that cry – the answer of faith in the living God *"who inhabits eternity"* (Isaiah 57:15). "I do not believe," I replied to my friend, "in a God created in my own image, but in the

God who has revealed himself in his only Son, Jesus Christ. A God of holiness and love who has promised to judge the world in righteousness but still offers men salvation through the cross."

If such a God were not eternal, he would be a fellow-prisoner with us, locked in time, subject to its limitations, vulnerable to its ravages, changeable, undependable, and unworthy of our trust and worship. He would just simply not be God.

But the Bible affirms his eternity. It declares that, *"from everlasting to everlasting"* he is God (Psalm 90:2), or as A .W. Tozer has transliterated it, "from vanishing point to vanishing point." Beyond the farthest horizons of our past or our future, God is and was and will be. He is the great *"I AM"* (Exodus 3:14), the self existent God who transcends all things – time and space and matter. Together with the eternal Son (John 1:1-3) and the eternal Holy Spirit (Hebrews 9:14) he dwells in triune glory in the far pavilions of everlastingness. The incredible "light years" of modern space technology are like old fashioned wooden school rulers set against these vast dimensions. They just cannot cope with it.

Yet, though God is "timeless" in his essential Divine nature, he is not remote from time. He created time when he created matter; he acts in time; he invades it with his love; he is above it and beyond it, yet he is dynamically in it. He "changes times and seasons" because he is their Lord – the hymn writer's "Potentate of Time"!

God's eternal nature is the only hope of the time-locked universe. His *"eternal power and Divine nature"* are seen not only in its creation (Romans 1:20) but in the fact that he will determine its end, folding it up as a man does an outworn garment (Hebrews 1:10-12). Men boast of their powers of nuclear destruction, but the future of the universe lies not in Beijing, New Delhi, or in Washington, but in the hands of him in whom *"all things hold together,"* (Colossians 1:17).

In God's eternity lies the source of our personal security, *"The eternal God is Thy refuge, and underneath are the everlasting arms,"*

(Deuteronomy 33:27). The "safety net" of God's loving mercy is stretched beneath those who trust him. And its ropes will never fray. He has declared that he has loved us with an everlasting love, (Jeremiah 31:3), he has made an everlasting covenant with us (Jeremiah 32:40, Hebrews 13:30) and brought us by grace into an everlasting kingdom (2 Peter 1:11). In him, through his only begotten Son, Jesus, we have everlasting life, (John 3:16).

Because he is before time, above time, beyond time and yet within time, our salvation rests on One who is unchanging and is totally secure: *"I am the Lord,"* he says, *"I do not change: therefore you are not consumed..."* (Malachi 3:6).

God is never subject to "moods", never affected by circumstances, *"he never grows tired or weary"* (Isaiah 40:28) is never taken by surprise at the turn of events. For in his eternal Being, past, present and future are an open book to him. A thousand years are but a day to him – or more surprisingly, a *"watch in the night"* (Psalm 90:40). In the midst of "Millennium madness" the church will do well to remember that, as far as God is concerned, another 1,000 years is the equivalent of a few hours' "night duty"! In the words of Corporal Jones of *Dad's Army*, "Don't panic!" Or, more theologically, in the words of Maimonides, the Jewish philosopher, "When God walks, his footsteps are often times centuries apart!" And those who wait for him mount up with wings (Isaiah 40:31). By the same token, Jesus is *"the same yesterday, today and forever"* (Hebrews 13:8). His eternal perfection means there can never be any change in him – perfection cannot be "improved", neither can it deteriorate: it is – well, perfect! Eternal being is not measured only by its length but by its quality. It is endless because it is flawless.

Locked in the time warp of his own proud self sufficiency, modern man has lost his sense of transcendence. His horizons are narrow, his hopes in tatters. The note of pessimism sounds like a death knell in the vivid imagery of Shelley's poem on *Immortality*; "Life, like a dome of many coloured glass, stains the white radiance of eternity, until Death tramples it to fragments."

That spiritual fragmentation is symbolized, tragically, in the confused assortment of religions, but the fault lines of moral and spiritual brokenness run across the whole landscape of human life in the political, economic and social inequalities that divide men, and in the personal heartbreak of fractured relationships and inner hopelessness.

No amount of optimism about "The Challenge of a New Millennium" can change the desperate state of our fallen world. Only *"repentance toward God and faith in our Lord Jesus Christ"* (Acts 20:21) can do so. Great political – or, for that matter, religious programmes cannot meet the need of the world.

The fragmentation of human life is the result of man's refusal to acknowledge the living God (Romans 1:18), and where God's revelation is ignored society disintegrates, people cast off restraint and go to pieces (see Proverbs 29:18 NIV). Only in Christ is there hope: *"For God was pleased to have all his fullness dwell in him, and through him to reconcile to himself all things…making peace through his blood, shed on the cross"* (Colossians 1:19 NIV). Only through the eternal Son of God can the broken fragments of a fallen world be restored, the ravages of time healed and the hope of eternal life be offered to sinners.

That is why we must proclaim him as "Lord of all being, throned afar," and as the Saviour who entered time in order to destroy death and *"bring life and immortality to light through the Gospel,"* (2Timothy 1:10). Our focus must be upon him. We must tell the world about him, and centre our worship on him.

## *Encounter with the Ineffable*

**"I** wonder," mused a colleague the other day, "how the words, 'Before the Ineffable appear' would fit the rhythms of most modern worship music?" Indeed, I thought, how many people would know what "Ineffable" means? In fact, to be honest, I checked the dictionary just to make sure I had got it right!

The line comes from the hymn, *Eternal Light*, the echoes of which are rarely heard today. The 4/2 time is too slow and "churchy" for most contemporary congregations, the words archaic and almost incomprehensible. But it is not simply the old-fashioned tune and words that seem out of favour with modern ears; the truth is that the theology of "Eternal Light" does not sit easily with the brash self-confident mood of much modern Evangelicalism.

Take the first verse:

> *Eternal Light! Eternal Light!*
> *How pure the soul must be,*
> *When, placed within Thy searching sight,*
> *It shrinks not, but, with calm delight,*
> *Can live and look on Thee!*

There is an awareness of "light unapproachable", of eyes burning with "searching sight", of an awesome majesty that is but a reflection of the visions of God's infinite glory revealed to the saints of the Old and New Testaments. It is the kind of atmosphere that made Isaiah cry out, *"Woe is me, for I am a man of unclean lips,"* and John on Patmos to fall prostrate before the incandescent glory of the risen Christ.

Yet the hymn, also talks of "calm delight" and living and looking upon the glory of the Lord. The next verse speaks of the exalted spirits that surround the throne, who can "bear the burning bliss" because they have "never known a fallen world like this." Once again, we are in the atmosphere of John's great vision of the throne of God in the book of Revelation, where the four living creatures, the white robed elders, and a vast multitude of angelic beings and redeemed men and women bow in constant songs of adoration and praise before the central throne of the universe.

It is this awareness of the awe-inspiring glory of God that makes Thomas Binney, the hymn writer, break out into words that express his overwhelming sense of unworthiness before such majesty, in the words of the third verse;

> *Oh, how can I, whose native sphere*
> *Is dark, whose mind is dim,*
> *Before the Ineffable appear,*
> *And on my naked spirit bear*
> *The uncreated beam?*

Stripped of all self sufficiency and humbled to the dust, he knows that he cannot face the painful, blinding light. Brought out of the subterranean depths of his natural moral habitat into the dancing light of the eternal splendours, he is overwhelmed. Language fails, because the name of him who sits upon the throne is "Ineffable" – "inexpressible, beyond comprehension, unutterable." There is, as it were, "silence in heaven", and in that silence he hears the voice divine saying, *"Be still, and know that I am God,"*

"Ineffable" may be an old, little used word, and it may be totally foreign language to most modern people, but its very obscurity is part of its meaning! It stands for a name so exalted, so beyond the reaches of human understanding, so awesome in its mystery, that it demands more than cold analysis – it demands the bowing of the heart, mind and will in breathless wonder. Here is no slick slogan sliding off the tongue with practised ease, this is *"the Name high over all"* the

Name of him who is *"glorious in holiness, fearful in praises, doing wonders"* (Exodus 15:11).

In Old Testament times, the people feared to use "Yahweh", the given Name of God, lest they should take the Name of the Lord in vain. The Name of God was indeed "Ineffable", it was wrapped in impenetrable mystery as fearful as the thunder and lightening that rocked Sinai when he came down to give the Law. They preferred to call him "Adonai" or "Elohim" rather than use that dreaded Name.

In our cosy familiarity with deity we are sometimes tempted to regard such fear as needless, even superstitious, but we may be in danger of losing a dimension of worship which will leave us spiritually impoverished.

Ours is the age of technology. We are good at the mechanics of worship but are in danger of losing its mystery. The worship industry sells us all we need in terms of resources – music, CD's, DVD's and seminars to teach us all the know-how of praise. With a little skill we can even synthesise singing in the Spirit, so that what once rose mysteriously and spontaneously from a congregation, like *"a mist from the earth"* in the Garden of Eden, is sometimes now produced by the worship leader singing persuasively into his microphone. Like modern preaching, much modern worship tends to be man-centred – evaluated by what it does to rather than by how God sees it. If it feels good it must be right, and if the Holy Spirit is rather slow to move on his own account, then we have the ways and means of helping him out. If the river of God doesn't flow we can still prime the pump.

"Ineffable" doesn't come into our vocabulary because it is transcendent and we like things to be down to earth, capable of analysis and easy to control. Mysticism is viewed with suspicion as an obsolete form of medieval monasticism, the quiet art of meditation is regarded as passive inactivity, and the "silence of eternity" as a waste of time. The manic rush of modern life takes us with accelerating pace here and there, cramming every moment with "productivity", urging us on to better performance and higher achievement, but leaving us with emptiness of heart and poverty of spirit. Like the child Samuel (1 Samuel 3:1, 7) we *"minister unto the Lord"* but yet *"do not know the Lord"*. It may well be that, like Samuel, we need afresh to hear the voice of the Lord we profess to serve and do not really know – and it may well be that it will take some dark night of the soul to make us hear that voice, and hearing, to tremble.

Just recently I stood with friends on the lower slopes of the Himalayas, at a point twice the height of Snowdon, and looked through the fir trees at other peaks twice the height again. Away in the distance, across the border with China, we could see other mountains, snow-capped and rising higher still, and we knew that in the far, unseen distances the great mass of Everest rose in all its awesome splendour. Compared with the hills and mountains we had known previously, our present situation was breathtaking, but we knew there were other heights lying beyond us, unexplored and full of glory. So it is in the spiritual realm. Yet so often we are content to wander the foothills of spiritual mediocrity when the voice of the Lord summons us to the mount. The tragedy is that we are not ready for the climb. C. Day Lewis has put it memorably,

> *Those Himalayas of the mind*
> *Are not so easily possessed;*
> *There's more than precipice and storm*
> *Between you and your Everest.*

Only a man with clean hands and a pure heart can *"ascend the hill of the Lord"*, and for some of us that price is too high and the effort too much. As John Oxenham put it,

> *To every man, there openeth*
> *A way, and ways, and a way;*

22

*And the high soul climbs the high way,*
*And the low soul treads the low;*
*And in between, on the misty flats,*
*The rest drift to and fro.*

Too many of us are simply that – spiritual drifters, content to wander on the lower levels because the demands of true fellowship with God are too costly. We know that *"without holiness no man shall see the Lord"*, but holiness demands radical soul surgery – it means dealing with some of the secret things that grieve the Spirit, cutting out the pride, the wrong attitudes, the questionable relationships, the critical spirit, the self-centeredness and the other things about which the Word and Spirit of God have been talking to us for a long time. It means facing the truth about ourselves and coming out into the open before God in humble repentance and obedient faith.

God give us the holy realism that will see our present spiritual state in true perspective, a holy desire for more of God, and a holy determination to keep on climbing, whatever that involves.

Thomas Binney does not leave us stranded and confused on some inaccessible mountain height. His magnificent hymn ends with a glorious certainty,

*There is a way for man to rise*
*To that sublime abode;*
*An offering and a sacrifice,*
*A Holy Spirit's energies,*
*An advocate with God.*
*These, these prepare us for the sight*
*Of holiness above;*
*The sons of ignorance and night*
*May dwell in the eternal light,*
*Through the eternal love!*

In Christ, the "Ineffable", the "wholly other", incomprehensible, invisible One, who "dwells in light unapproachable" has made himself known. On the Mount of Transfiguration he throws the full beam of revelation upon Jesus and declares, *"This is my beloved Son. Hear him!"* It is Christ who has made known the unknowable, he is the *"unspeakable gift"* (2 Corinthians 9:15), he is *"the image of the invisible God"* (Colossians 1:15); in him are hidden God's *"unsearchable riches"* (Ephesians 3:8), and through him we encounter love that *"passes knowledge"* and power that soars far above the most extravagant flights of our imagination (Ephesians 3:19,20). In Christ we whisper the "Ineffable Name," and though we do but partly understand, in him we rejoice – with *"joy unspeakable (ineffable) and full of glory"* (1 Peter 1:8).

Real worship is not the end-product of a cleverly polished technique – it is the gasp of wonder at the glory of the Lord.

## *The Extravagance of God*

The man on the radio said it, quoting a poet whose name I did not catch, but the words caught my attention: "the extravagant kindnesses of God." Of course I knew that God was kind, even at school when we learned the Ten Commandments (I wish they did it now). I knew that he *"showed mercy unto thousands"*, and when as a teenager I read the Bible for myself I discovered that it was crammed full of the *"steadfast love of the Lord"*, something that personal experience would prove again and again.

The hymn writers, with their wonderful way of taking up truths and working them into logical sequences, helped me to gain new insight into this loving kindness of God. To quote just one,

> *For the love of God is broader*
> *Than the measure of man's mind;*
> *And the heart of the Eternal*
> *Is most wonderfully kind.*

But still that word "extravagant" fascinated me – and set me thinking.

"God is extravagant"! In modern terms, he "goes over the top"! He doesn't do things by halves. When he gives us the gift of his Son it is an *"indescribable gift"* – a gift "beyond words" (2Corinthians 9:15 NIV), a gift that comes to us out of the *"incomparable riches of his grace"* (Ephesians 2:7) and is composed of the *"unsearchable riches of Christ"* (Ephesians 3:8). He wants us to experience the *"exceeding greatness of his power"* in our human lives (Ephesians 1:19) and assures us that he is *"able to do immeasurably more than all we ask or imagine, according to his power that is at work within us"* (Ephesians 3:20). He wants us to know the love of Christ *"which surpasses knowledge"* so that, incredibly, our poor shrivelled lives might be *"filled with all the fullness of God"* (Ephesians 3:19). And he doesn't stop there! He promises us *"joy unspeakable and full of glory"* (1Peter 1:8). Oh my! The superlatives soar above us like Himalayan peaks towering into infinity, *"For as the heavens are higher than the earth, so are my ways higher than your ways, and my thoughts than your thoughts,"* says the Lord (Isaiah 55:9). Amazing though it seems, even accelerating sin is overtaken by supercharged grace (Romans 5:20). Another "much more"!

God's extravagant kindnesses are seen in creation. Paul reminds an audience of pagans in Lystra that the Creator-God *"has shown kindness by giving you rain from heaven and crops in their seasons; he provides you with plenty of food and fills your hearts with joy"* (Acts 14:17,18). As the Lord Jesus said, our heavenly Father does that for the unrighteous as well as the righteous (Matthew 5:45). Paul repeats the same idea when reminding us that God *"generously gives us everything for our enjoyment"* (1Timothy 6:17 J.B.Phillips).

So creation is more than a highly organized machine supervised by some celestial technocrat from a remote cosmic control centre: it is more a work of art, God's gift to us, designed not merely to sustain our existence but to make us happy. It is full of exciting shapes and colours; it is a "touchy-feely" world of textures and tastes which our senses can explore with continual surprise: it is a world of sound orchestrated by the God who made the morning stars sing at its creation and still conducts the dawn chorus every day.

God might have provided our vitamin intake in the form of monotonous grey tablets – instead, he gave them to us in a riot of colour and taste – carrots and peas, oranges, bananas, raspberries and plums, the list is endless. And, glory to God, even cabbage is green! It might have been brown.

He might have made the world as a strictly functional environment, simply there to sustain life; instead, "deep in unfathomable mines of never failing skill, he treasures up his bright designs and works his sovereign will." In the alchemy of sovereign goodness he transmutes

26

dust particles into the gold of stunning sunsets, takes rain drops and turns them into multicoloured rainbows – and the darker the sky, the brighter they glow. He grows secret gardens of exquisite underwater coral, playfully hides iridescent shells beneath the sand of the seashore and shares the happiness of the children who find the buried treasure. He not only adorns the aristocratic rose but raises weeds to the peerage by setting golden coronets on dandelions, and trails his coat of many colours along the hedgerows of country lanes, and amid the rubble of city building sites. In his extravagant kindness he wants us not only to exist, but to live joyously in a world of unutterable beauty. He welcomes spring with a fanfare of daffodils and sends tulips marching through the park like red coated guardsmen on parade.

"The world is charged with the grandeur of God," cried Gerard Manley Hopkins, and went on to reflect that, "there lives the dearest freshness deep down things." And why? "Because the Holy Ghost over the bent world broods with warm breast and ah! Bright wings."

It is a world that invites our admiration, demands our respect, and points us to him who made it for his own glory and our enjoyment, and who calls us to be equally generous in our response (1 Timothy 6:18,19).

*"I will sing of the kindnesses of the Lord,"* calls Isaiah 63:7-14, in a passage that celebrates *"the many good things He has done for the house of Israel according to his compassion and many kindnesses."* He becomes their Saviour, enters so deeply into their situation that he himself becomes distressed by their distresses; he redeems them, lifts them up and carries them like a father does a tired and fretful child, and even when they rebel against him he still does not utterly reject them, but after disciplining them continues to lead them as a shepherd does his flock, bringing them through the Red Sea and giving them rest by his Holy Spirit in the land he has selected for them.

For Israel, the kindnesses of God are extravagant in as much as they are wholly undeserved. This was a nation chosen, not for its inherent greatness or superior spirituality, but by the sovereign grace of God: *"The Lord did not set his affection on you and choose you because you were more numerous than other peoples, for you were the fewest of all people. But it was because the Lord loved you and kept the oath he swore to your forefathers,"* (Deuteronomy 7:7,8). In fact, the first of those "forefathers", Abraham, was a moon-worshipping pagan in Ur of the Chaldees! This was no high-born master-race tracing its ancestry back to unblemished blood, but a nomadic tribe which had to confess, *"My father was a wandering Aramean"* (Deuteronomy 26:5).

Only extravagant grace raised its profiles. All through the turbulent history of Israel the kindnesses of God shine forth. He takes a quarrelsome family of restless travellers, forges them into nationhood on the anvil of persecution in Egypt, leads them out of bondage by a mighty act of deliverance, *"suffers their* (appalling) *manners in the wilderness"* (Acts 13:18), brings them into a lush land of promise and with astonishing patience bears with their repeated rebellions until at last he brings, reluctantly, his judgment upon them. And even then he promises them future restoration, sending forth his only Son as the promised Messiah.

And that is where we come in. Listen to Paul in Ephesians 2:6,7 *"And God raised us up with Christ and seated us with him in the heavenly realms in Christ Jesus, in order that in the coming ages he might show the incomparable riches of his grace, expressed in his kindness to us in Christ Jesus."* Or listen to him in Titus 3:4-6: *"But when the kindness and love of God appeared, he saved us, not because of righteous things we had done, but because of His mercy. He saved us through the washing of rebirth and the renewal of the Holy Spirit, whom he poured out on us generously through Jesus Christ our Saviour."*

*"The kindness of God"*. The emotive words occur only once in that form in the Old Testament, in the story of David and Mephibosheth (2 Samuel 9). Magnanimous in victory, David desires to *"show the kindness of God"* towards Saul's family. But Mephibosheth is the only survivor of the bloodbath that engulfed his family, and he himself is crippled. His self esteem is at an all time low: *"I am a dead dog,"* he says, but that's where the kindness of God shines brightest! This man belonged to a doomed family, he himself was severely damaged, a no hoper; but in an act of sheer grace he is restored to the royal palace, granted the privileges of the king's table and assured of complete protection and provision for his future.

This is but a human example of what God has done for us in Christ: *"As for you, you were dead in transgressions and sins...you followed the ways of this world and of... the spirit who is now at work among those who are disobedient...Like the rest we were by nature objects of wrath. But...God who is rich in mercy made us alive with Christ even when we were dead in transgressions...And God raised us up with Christ and seated us with Him in the heavenly realms"* (Ephesians 2:1-6).

Like Mephibosheth, we are not merely forgiven and tolerated; we are brought to the king's table, made to share in the benefits of his triumphs and given an inheritance that is imperishable. Or like the returning prodigal, we are not given the servile status which was the best we dared hope for, but we stagger backward under the onrush of the Father's passionate embrace and find ourselves overwhelmed by the amazing lavishness of his kindness to us. *"You have been washed, you have been sanctified, you have been justified in the name of the Lord Jesus Christ,"* says Paul (1 Corinthians 6:11). The sin-stained rags are gone, there's a new look to us – a robe of righteousness, shoes on our flint – cut feet, a golden ring of royal status on fingers that had grubbed in desperation amongst the pig swill, and heaven dancing for joy.

*"How great is the love that the Father has lavished upon us, that we should be called the children of God! And that is what we are!"* (1 John 4:1). So why is it that so many of the returning prodigals look more like the grumpy elder brother than joyous, forgiven sinners? Why don't more of us join the party? Why are there so many grim faced, critical, unresponsive Christians standing on the edge of things? Why do we seem to think that aloofness is a sign of spiritual refinement, that emotion is always "dangerous emotionalism" to be avoided in the name of spiritual correctness?

If God is so extravagant in creation and redemption, shouldn't we be extravagant in thankful worship, generous giving, loving fellowship and dedicated service? If he pours millions of gallons into rivers, splashes colour everywhere, lavishly scatters stars across the universe, takes a moon-worshipping idolater and makes him the father of a great nation, and most of all, sends his only Son to save a wicked world – a Son who is willing to leave the pristine glory of heaven, come down the stairway of time and share the appalling filth of the human slum and pour out his blood in saving grace – shouldn't we join his celebrations? And, since he has been so kind to us, shouldn't we be extravagantly kind to each other? Actually, that's the "dress code" for the party: *"Be kind and compassionate to one another, forgiving each other. Just as in Christ God forgave you"* (Ephesians 4:32). Maybe that's why a lot of Christians look awkward and out of place in church. Maybe we ought to start dressing and living to please our heavenly Father – extravagantly!

## *The Worship God is Looking For*

Luxurious furniture, cordon bleu food and drink, exotic cosmetics, and the latest in contemporary music were the hallmarks of the upmarket society in the days of Amos (6:4-6). It was a time of easy-going complacency, and – as so often happens – the spirit of the age had infiltrated the church. Pleased with a religious enthusiasm which was also relevant to the contemporary world, they were supremely confident that they were preparing for the great "new day" God would soon usher in (Amos 5:18).

But they were wrong! God was not at all happy with their version of contemporary worship. In some of the most disturbing words in the Bible he exposed the truth about the worship they thought was so good: *"I hate all your show and pretence – the hypocrisy of your religious festivals and solemn assemblies... Away with your hymns of praise! They are only noise to my ears. I will not listen to your music, no matter how lovely it is,"* (Amos 5:21-23, NLT). The *Message* version is even stronger: *"I can't stand your religious meetings. I'm fed up with your conferences and conventions...I've had enough of your noisy ego-music. When was the last time you to sang to me?"*

The rugged, rustic shepherd – vine-dresser – prophet from Tekoa cut through the sophisticated enthusiasms of contemporary religion to reveal its failure in the eyes of the Lord. God wanted more than nice music and impressive religious events; he called for holiness, righteousness and social justice (Amos 5:24).

The vital connection between how we behave in church and what we are in daily life is emphasised in the words of Jesus in Matthew 15:8, 9. Quoting the words of Isaiah 29:13, he declared, *"These people honour me with their lips, but their hearts are far from me. They worship me in vain; their teachings are but rules taught by men."* It is possible to develop an impressive format of worship, whether traditional or contemporary in style, but unless the lifestyle of the worshippers resonates with their liturgy it becomes like *"a noisy gong or a clanging cymbal"*, supremely irritating to the ears of God.

When the woman of Samaria tried to begin an evasive debate about "comparative religion", Jesus quickly pointed out to her that God was not concerned with the location or liturgy of worship, but with the heart condition of the worshippers (John 4:19-24). The Father, he said, *"seeks* (is earnestly looking for) *those who will worship him in spirit and in truth."* Kenneth Wuest in his *Expanded Translation* renders the passage in a helpful way: "God as to his nature is spirit, and for those who are worshipping, it is necessary in the nature of the case to be worshipping in a spiritual sphere, and in the sphere of truth." In other words, true worship is not confined to musical or outward forms of expression; it is supremely a spiritual encounter with God in which mind meets mind, spirit engages with spirit, heart beats with heart, an encounter that only takes place when the Holy Spirit becomes the divine go-between, enabling God and the worshipper to draw near to one another in a meaningful relationship.

Such worship moves, as Wuest puts it, "in the sphere of truth". It is not a response to the rhythm of a new song or the nostalgic sound of a well-loved hymn; in fact, it is not dependent on music at all, but on pondering the revelation of God's glory and grace in his Word. True worship is contemplative, it is aroused by "surveying" the wondrous cross, by putting together, as the psalmist did in Psalm 45:1, heart-stirring and tongue-loosening truths about the glory of Christ in his personal splendour and sovereign power (vv 2-8). Moreover, moving "in the sphere of truth" has a profound effect on the personal life of the worshipper. It requires more than theological correctness, it demands integrity, honesty, and a humble openness to the searching Spirit of him who requires *"clean hands and a pure heart"* in those who wish to stand in his holy place (Psalm 24:3-6).

## *Let's Forget about Ourselves and Worship Jesus*

I had the privilege of conducting a Bible study series on "The Throne of Destiny" at my home church in Leeds. As we looked at the throne of God through the eyes of Isaiah, Ezekiel, Daniel and John, I was deeply challenged afresh by the transcendent sovereignty, glorious majesty, overwhelming power, breath-taking beauty and awesome holiness of God, and by the captivating wonder of his grace and mercy.

Truly, "our God is an awesome God!" But it is easy to sing those words quite jauntily without really grasping the implications of what we are singing. I was gripped by the awe-inspiring visions of God and the wonder of his throne – the storm clouds, the roll of thunder and the flashing lightning, the strange celestial beings, the dazzling, jewel-studded colours, the enveloping flames of fire, the sheen of glowing metal, the august figure of the Ancient of Days, the majesty of the Son of Man and the mystery of the Lion-Lamb. But more than that, I was deeply challenged and inspired by the worship that rolled, wave after wave, towards the throne.

Challenged, because of the comparison between this sublime worship and what often passes for worship in our modern churches, and inspired to catch something of the heavenly ethos of real worship.

Challenged, because the most exalted beings in the universe – the seraphim and cherubim – cover their faces with their wings in deep reverence before this exalted majesty. And because the twenty four elders – representing the highest echelons of authority amongst men – vacate their thrones, throw down their crowns – symbolic of human leadership – and prostrate themselves in total subservience and unrestrained worship before the majesty of God and the glory of the Lamb.

There is no light-hearted familiarity here, no levity, no seeking for position, no attempt to win recognition or gain influence, no posturing, no eye-catching "performance ministry", nothing but an overwhelming sense of the incandescent fire of God's eternal holiness and the encircling rainbow of his grace.

In his book *The Trivialization of God*, Donald McCullough writes: "Our joyous gratitude, we discover, has led us into the throne room of the universe, and now we are in the presence of the Holy One who utterly transcends us, who holds together all creation from the smallest molecule to the largest galaxy and all history from the first page to the last, who is burning in wrath against sin with the flame of purging love, who has claimed us in Jesus Christ and will keep us in the embrace of grace for all eternity."

Our brash, self-confident, sometimes flippant, generation needs to realise that there is only one thing to do in the presence of such glory: bow down in godly fear and worship as he desires – *"in Spirit and in truth"* (John 4:23, 24), trusting only in his grace.

I am challenged, too, and moved by the God-centred, Christ-exalting, Spirit-inspired songs that echo round the throne. In contrast to so much of modern worship, there are virtually no personal pronouns in the songs in the book of Revelation, the focus is never on the worshippers, their feelings or even their aspirations, only on God himself: "The Lamb is all the glory in Emmanuel's land."

To quote Donald McCullough again: "Sometimes what passes for worship is more human-centred than God-centred. We want to make sure everyone 'gets something' out of the experience... But what difference does it make if God is not at the centre? What we really need when we show up for worship is for our attention to be turned toward the glory of God."

When Matt Redman sings of "coming back to the heart of worship", he reminds us of the most important thing – "it's all about you, Jesus, all about you." Only in that frame of mind and heart can we worship in the way that pleases God. As an older song put it: "Let's forget about ourselves and concentrate on him and worship him."

## *Reaching the Ultimate Point of Worship*

It was 4am and dark. Making his way home after his shift in the mine, he saw lights on in the chapel and thinking there must be an intruder, went to investigate. He was no "chapel person"; indeed, like Saul of Tarsus, he was "a blasphemer and a persecutor and a violent man". Nonetheless, it was the least he could do.

He reached the pine-clad porch of the chapel and discovered there *was* an intruder – a divine one! Inside the chapel there rose the sound of singing, but here in the vestibule he was suddenly overcome by an awesome sense of the presence of a holy God. He stood transfixed, not daring to move. He was afraid to enter the chapel because he knew God was in there; he was afraid to step into the darkness outside because it seemed to hold some unknown horror. Eventually, he pushed open the chapel door and amid the prayers and songs of a revival meeting threw himself on the mercy of God.

This Welsh miner had experienced what Jacob felt when he cried, *"Surely the Lord is in this place and I was not aware of it...How awesome is this place! This is none other than the house of God; this is the gate of heaven"* (Genesis 28:16, 17).

That the manifest presence of God should be made known to two such men who were personally undeserving of it is a reminder of the fact that every such manifestation is a sovereign act of divine grace. It can neither be earned nor manufactured.

It is, of course, wonderfully true that Wesley's deathbed cry, "Best of all, God is with us", is a fact of everyday life for us as Christians, and that the promise of Jesus to be with his people *"where two or three are gathered together"* is always fulfilled; but it is also true that there are moments when the sense of the presence of God seems specially and awesomely real, times when the sense of his holiness creates a deep awareness of personal unworthiness and repentance for sin (Acts 5:11); times when the revelation of his glory moves us on a

35

surging floodtide of worship; times when we cry, "Surely the Lord is in this place!" and times when even our worship and ministry are silenced in the presence of his transcendent majesty (2 Chronicles 5:13, 14).

Why are such moments relatively rare? Granted that their occurrence is determined by the sovereignty of God, but can it also be because we are so taken up with busily running our lives and our churches that the Lord has little opportunity to break in amongst us? Is it because we are content to experience a pleasurable degree of "blessing" in our worship and ministry but rarely hunger and thirst for more of God? Is it because, almost unconsciously, we feel we can create the sense of God's presence by the way we plan and conduct our meetings, by our choice of songs and methods of ministry?

Psalm 33:1-3 encourages us to seek to excel vocally and instrumentally, to be innovative and enthusiastic in our worship, and we can rejoice in the latest "worship technology" which enables us to achieve higher standards; but we must never be content with achieving just that. Our enjoyment of the journey of worship may actually prevent us from reaching our destination – the essential encounter with God himself. Our praise and worship styles may have become more advanced, but some of us need to remember that, to paraphrase Zechariah's famous text (4:6), it is "not by 'hype' nor by 'power point,' *but by my Spirit, says the Lord"*. Our goal must be God himself (Psalm 42:1, 2).

We cannot manufacture the presence of God, but we can constantly seek it and prepare for it. Isaiah urges us to *"prepare the way for the Lord; make straight in the wilderness a highway for our God"*, to be satisfied with nothing less, to do everything necessary to remove the obstacles that get in God's way, both personally and collectively, so that *"the glory of the Lord will be revealed"* (40:3-5). And that is something special. It's the ultimate point of worship which, strangely, lies beyond "worship"!

## *The Parable of the Northern Lights*

The actress Joanna Lumley lifted her eyes heavenward and whispered, "Thank you, thank you!" To whom she was offering such heartfelt thanks was not certain. It may indeed have been to God; on the other hand, it may have been to "mother nature" or some other "unknown god". One thing is certain, however: she had been deeply moved by one of the most impressive displays of beauty in the universe. She was in Tromso, in Norway, presenting an absorbing TV documentary about the mysterious Northern Lights in which a breathtaking sequence of ever-changing colours – glorious shades of green and blue, pink and red – hung from beneath a starlit sky like great curtains of light draped over the northern horizon and swirling in constantly altering patterns of shape and size as they were blown by a powerful solar wind.

Although we lived in the south of England, I have rare memories of watching the aurora borealis glowing over the edges of the Hampshire hills with a mysterious, almost eerie beauty. In fact, they filled my youthful mind with a kind of fascinated dread, and to this day the words Northern Lights still cause a strange frisson of awe, almost akin to fear, to ripple through me.

Joanna Lumley gave thanks to "someone out there", Yeats waxed eloquent about "the embroidered cloth of heaven, enwrought with gold and silver light", Wordsworth's "heart leaped up" when he "beheld a rainbow in the sky", Keats sang an *Ode to a Nightingale*, Turner painted stunning sunsets, Debussy wrote the silvery loveliness of *Claire de Lune*, and a host of poets, songwriters, composers and painters have been and are inspired by what they see in nature. The sad thing is that many of them only see nature; the glory of the Creator is unknown to them. They praise his works but never worship him.

They are not alone. Too many people are so taken up with their environment, with the day-to-day demands of life, and some even with what they call "my work for God", that they have lost God in the encircling fog of their personal preoccupation with what Jesus called *"life's worries, riches and pleasures"* (Luke 8:14). Some have even lost him on the mountain paths of "blessing"! They are more impressed by what he does for them than who he is.

The men of the Bible had no such limitations. To them, the *"heavens declare the glory of God, the skies proclaim the work of his hands"* (Psalm 19:1). As Paul puts it, *"Since the creation of the world God's invisible qualities – his eternal power and divine nature – have been clearly seen from what has been made"* (Romans 1:20). Furthermore, the universe not only declares his creative genius but also his moral splendour: *"The heavens proclaim his righteousness"* (Psalm 50:6). Their continuing existence, in spite of man's rebellion, through the unending succession of the regular seasons of the year are the token of his faithfulness (Genesis 8:21,22) and utter dependability (Malachi 3:6).

The stars that span the heavens have not been mass produced on some vast cosmic production line, they have been individually crafted by a divine jeweller who numbers them and knows them by name and has placed them into a magnificent galactic "necklace" suspended from the heavens: they are *"the work of God's fingers"*(Psalm 8:3; 102:25; Isaiah 40:26). In the same way, the awesome Northern Lights are not merely a natural phenomenon, they are created by *"the Father of the heavenly lights who does not change like shifting shadows"* (James 1:17), and *"out of the north comes golden splendour; God is clothed with awesome majesty"* (Job 37:22, ESV).

The God who creates rainbows out of raindrops, and sunsets out of refracted light shining through a dusty evening haze, can also move solar particles into an invasion of earth's atmosphere and through that interaction of heaven and earth create the breathtaking beauty of the Northern Lights. Surely, there's a parable there.

Yes, indeed, "Thank you, thank you – dear heavenly Father!"

# The Word Made Flesh

# *Reflections*

## *Bethlehem's "Door of Destiny"*

It was probably rusty, maybe lacking a screw or two, and almost certainly attached to third-grade, splintered wood. But it was, in the words of American preacher Ralph Sockman, "the hinge of history" on the door of a Bethlehem stable.

In contrast to the pomp and pageantry of kings and presidents and the sleek, purring cavalcades of limousines conveying world leaders to their summits – and, sadly, to the ostentation of many of the Lord's 21st century "servants" – the entrance of the Son of God into the world was markedly low-key. As Phillips Brooks sang, "How silently, how silently, the wondrous gift is given!" There was, however, a host of angels pouring from Bethlehem's skies in a cascade of song, but that was a private "Christmas card" for a few lonely shepherds. The world at large heard nothing – the Messiah slipped unobtrusively from eternity into time. The words of another poem sum up the paradox of the incarnation of Jesus,

> *They were all looking for a king*
> *To lead them forth and lift them high.*
> *He came a little baby thing*
> *That made a woman cry.*

But that, so often, is God's way of doing things. Micah reminds us that Bethlehem had no particular claim to fame: it was *"little among the thousands of Judah"* (Micah 5:2). But out of that unimportant place came a ruler whose roots were in eternity. Nathanael asked, *"Can any good thing come out of Nazareth?"* (John 1:46) and others said, *"You won't find a prophet coming from a place like that!"* (John 7:52). But out of that run-down town, came the Saviour of the world.

The Apostle Paul would never have made it on the God Channel. They said, *"He's a good writer, but he lacks personality and he's no good as a preacher!"* (2 Corinthians 10:10 – my "translation"). Yet this was the man God used to shape the theology and inspire the worship of the church throughout all time.

It is always dangerous to judge people or places by outward appearance. So often God chooses and uses foolish things, weak things, lowly things, despised things and "nothings" to demolish the arrogance of the world (1 Corinthians 1:26f). Once again we learn that, in God's eyes, "substance is far more important than image."

The world imagines that it can shape history and create security by erecting impressive and loudly trumpeted political and economic structures (super-states and globalisation). It should study the story of the tower of Babel (Genesis 11)! Sometimes the Church seems to think it can bring in the kingdom through loudly acclaimed structures and methods. However, it should remember that *"the kingdom of God is not a matter of talk but of power"* (1 Corinthians 4:20). It is not about creating a brand image, or high-flown rhetoric about dynamic leadership, cutting-edge ministry, and prophetic this and that, but about humility and actual empowerment by the Spirit.

History does indeed turn on that rough-edged stable door in Bethlehem. More precisely, it revolves around the Incarnation of Jesus Christ – his virgin birth, his sinless life, his atoning death, his glorious resurrection and his ascension to the throne of the universe – in which he triumphed over the powers of darkness and wrested the keys of human destiny from the grip of the devil. God has made him both Lord and Christ. The great Scottish preacher James S Stewart has summed it up superbly, "A child is born to a peasant woman; a young man toils at a bench; half a dozen fishermen suddenly leave their boats... In the obscurity of a wooded glade a bowed figure wrestles in prayer; on an insignificant hill a cross is raised; in a garden a tomb stands empty. It all sounds so local... far removed from the rushing years and the surge and thunder of the deeds of men... Yet it is this that in the providence of God has leapt the barriers of the centuries and the frontiers of every nation under heaven. It is this that from its hidden beginnings has stormed the mind and conscience of the world..." It's true – that creaking old door in Bethlehem opens up a whole new world!

## Pentecost at Christmas

In Rome, Caesar Augustus casually scrawled his signature on a census document that would disrupt the lives of millions of his subjects across the empire. In Nazareth, a humble carpenter and his pregnant wife left home to register in the place of their ancestral roots – 80 miles away. In the midnight blue of an eastern sky, a star of astonishing brilliance flashed a message that triggered the wise mens' expedition in search of a royal baby. Over Bethlehem, a cascade of singing angels poured from heaven in a display of sound and light that propelled a group of frightened shepherds in a search for the Saviour of the world. In Jerusalem, a puppet king, half-Jew, half-Arab, listened with mounting alarm to ancient prophecies telling of a coming true-born son of David, and brooded over a plan to exterminate him.

This complex pattern of Roman politics, Jewish history, intimate personal experience and divine purpose made Bethlehem the epicentre of an event which would shake the foundations of human history and transform the moral and spiritual landscape of the world. And beyond this fascinating interplay of human actions and divine purposes lay the hidden but dynamic work of the Holy Spirit. In fact, without him there would have been no Christmas story, no incarnation, no cross, no resurrection, no ascended, reigning Lord, no coming King, no Gospel, and no church to preach it! Guardedly and reverently, we may say that the whole plan of redemption depended on the Holy Spirit.

Behind the drama of the first Christmas, the Spirit worked mysteriously and creatively in the body of a village girl (Luke 1:35 cf Matthew 1:20, 21), and in the life of her aged cousin, Elizabeth, giving her a son when all hope had gone forever. By his presence Elizabeth and her husband Zechariah were *"filled with the Spirit"* and broke out into prophecy, and Mary sang an inspired worship song

(Luke 1:41-55,67-79). Meanwhile, the Spirit was upon the aged Simeon, granting him special revelation about the Messiah's birth, and leading him into the temple at the precise moment when Jesus was presented before God. He, too, was enabled to prophesy under the Spirit's anointing (Luke 2:25-35), and the 84 year-old widow Anna, the prophetess, was enabled to *"give thanks to God and speak of him* (Jesus) *to all who were waiting for redemption"* (Luke 2:36-38).

God's secret agent was at work beneath and within and beyond the world of political power-seeking, social upheaval and religious confusion, bringing about supernatural happenings in individual human lives in terms of creation, inspiration, revelation, and direction. This was world-changing "Pentecost" at Christmas!

The journey of the Magi is a reminder to us that neither wealth nor wisdom need necessarily stop God from working in us, while Zechariah and Elizabeth, Joseph and Mary, Simeon and Anna tell us that *"the secret of the Lord is with them that fear him"* in humble openness to the Spirit, faith, and sincerity of heart.

Within the complexity of the modern world, we need to understand that only the Holy Spirit can bring about the purposes of God, and that he does so in the lives of ordinary people who are willing to say with Mary, *"I am the Lord's servant, and I am willing to accept whatever he wants"* (Luke 1:38 NLT). Or, as we used to sing, "Here I am, wholly available!"

## *Don't Ignore the Neighbour from Heaven!*

"**W**ill God really dwell on earth with men?" The question falls from Solomon's lips as he stands before the great temple he has built. His eyes sweep over its spacious courts and massive pillars, and he sees the towering majesty of its soaring architecture, then he lifts his gaze beyond the highest pinnacle to where the great blue dome of heaven arches over it all and is overawed by its vastness. This great temple, created by the wealth of the richest man in the world and the artistry of the wisest man in the world, is dwarfed by the universe in which it stands; and he knows when darkness falls that same dome will be lit by millions of star lamps glittering from immeasurable distances, and far beyond them, mysteriously vast, will be the far pavilions of "the heaven of heavens." He is overwhelmed with the staggering contrast (2 Chronicles 6:18). God, on earth? Living with men? Unthinkable!

How, indeed, can you localise the infinite? How can you harmonise the incompatible – bridge separation between a holy God and a rebellious race? How can you verbalise the inexpressible – translate the free-flowing poetry of eternal truth into the stilted prose of human speech? To man "come of age" in a world of radio telescopes and space probes, the realisation of the size of the universe creates a problem which is even more staggering. Man's greatest explorations are nothing more than riding a fairy cycle round the backyard, and his search for secrets in the cosmos like digging holes in the beach in the hope of capturing the ocean. Moreover, such knowledge as he does have fills him with a sense of his own insignificance and vulnerability. As modern poet Edward Shillito put it,

> *The heavens frighten us; they are too calm.*
> *In all the universe we have no place.*
> *Our wounds are hurting us; where is the balm?*
> *Lord Jesus, by thy scars we claim thy grace.*

The answer to that cry for help – and to Solomon's question – lies in John 1:14: *"The Word became flesh and dwelt among us."*

The incredible thing has taken place! In the person of his Son, who as "the Word" (Logos) is the perfect expression of his infinite glory, God has stepped down into time and revealed himself to fallen men. In Jesus Christ, he *"became flesh and dwelt among us"* (John1:14) – *"moved into the neighbourhood"* (*The Message*), pitched his tent in our squalid encampment and shared our limitations; *"He who was rich became poor for our sakes"* (2 Corinthians 5:21) – he who had lived eternally amidst the mountain freshness of the uplands of heaven came down into the fetid atmosphere of earth and then, fragrant in personal holiness, waded into the filth-laden sewer of human degradation to unblock the massive build-up of sin, guilt and shame that separated us from God; he whose slightest gesture moved squadrons of angels into instant action himself *"became obedient unto death, and that the death of the cross"* (Philippians 2:8) in order to give us life eternal.

God has "moved into the neighbourhood," but the sad thing is that, like the first Christmas, many of us don't seem to want to have much to do with the man who has come to live next door (John 1:10-12). It's time to invite him in (Revelation 3:20).

## The Dark Side of Christmas

As fog swirled down a deserted London street in the winter of 1741, an elderly German immigrant paused for breath outside a church. He was frail, suffering the effects of a near-fatal stroke some four years earlier, nearly bankrupt, frustrated by recent failures as a composer, and forsaken by his friends. As the church loomed through the gloom he thought about God, but it brought him no comfort, only questions: "Why did he grant me a renewal of my life," he whispered, "if I may no longer be permitted to create?"

In the hallway of his shabby lodgings, a bulky packet awaited his return. It was the libretto of a sacred oratorio prepared by his friend, Charles Jennens. He was in no mood for music, however, and scarcely gave the pages any attention as he turned them over. Then, suddenly, words leapt from the script: *"He was despised and rejected of men, a man of sorrows and acquainted with grief."* Powerfully, they resonated in his troubled soul and he turned to the rest of the verses Jennens had collated from the Bible. By now his mind was on fire, and for 24 days, his sleep abandoned and his food untouched, he wrote almost non-stop as some of the most glorious music ever written poured from his fast-moving pen.

Multitudes of musicians will take part in performances of Handel's *Messiah* every Christmas, and thousands more sit entranced by his inspired music, but how many understand the darkness and despair out of which it was born? Perhaps not many. In the same way, millions will celebrate Christmas once again, but how many will understand the dark realities out of which the Messiah – the Son of God and Saviour of men – was born? Again, not many.

To start with, neither Nazareth nor Bethlehem were the kind of places in which you'd expect to find anything worth looking for. Nazareth was a town with a bad reputation (John 1:46), and Bethlehem, in Helmut Thielicke's words, was a "one-horse town", a non-descript suburb of Jerusalem, *"too little to be among the clans of Judah"* (Micah 5:2, ESV). Furthermore, a small-time carpenter and his wife, about whose pregnancy there must have been suspicious rumours, were not the kind of people you'd expect to have any importance. They were just ordinary people caught up in a mass shift of population ordered by the authorities, having no clout in the fight for accommodation in a crowded town; they were just faceless statistics, mere numbers on a census form. And their baby? Just another little crying scrap of humanity destined for poverty and pain.

The taste of fear that made Mary tremble as the labour pains began in Bethlehem's stable would be nothing compared with the overwhelming sword-thrust of anguish which would engulf her at Calvary, and the cries that rose from the manger would be nothing compared to the searing pain that awaited this baby as he grew to manhood and trod the way to the cross. If there were shadows in the stable, there was "the horror of a great darkness" at Calvary.

Handel's *Messiah* is inspired by *"a man of sorrows"*, but it ends with a *Hallelujah Chorus* and a King who *"reigns for ever and ever"*. God's Messiah, born in the poverty-stricken anonymity of Bethlehem's stable, rises from his Easter tomb in final triumph and ascends to his Father's throne with a Name that reverberates through the universe with the ring of absolute power and glory. Out of the darkness, light shines.

It is that "dark side" of grace that takes a bigoted Pharisee like Saul of Tarsus – *"a blasphemer and a persecutor and a violent man"* (1Timothy 1:13) – and transforms him into one of the greatest Christians who ever lived, a grace that still moves with transforming power into the dark places of a fallen world where fear reigns, hope dies, unanswered questions haunt the mind, and all seems lost. It is this "dark side of Christmas" that brings it into touch with the harsh realities of life, where suffering and sin cast deep shadows that fairy lights and shining baubles can never banish.

To such a world Jesus came at Christmas, the *"light of the world"*, the "second Adam to the fight and rescue"; a Saviour who, because he shared our human situation and died in our stead, is able to *"save to the uttermost"* and make hope blaze in the darkness. That is why John writes, *"The light shines in the darkness, and the darkness can never extinguish it"* (John 1:5, NLT) – because it is *"the light of the glory of God in the face of Jesus Christ"* (2 Corinthians 4:6).

# The Christmas Dilemma:
## "Silent Night" or "Hark the Herald Angels Sing"?

Some time ago the musical world was thrown into controversy by a composition that required the orchestra to sit in silence for four minutes and 33 seconds. During that time, the only sound was caused by the musicians turning the blank pages of their "scores" and, probably, by the audience shifting uneasily in their seats.

Hailed by some, predictably, as innovative or avant-garde, it was generally dismissed as a piece of musical fraud. What the "composer" had in mind is not clear. It might conceivably have been a protest against the emptiness of the contemporary world; on the other hand, it might have been a cry for help against the endless noise that explodes all around us. In that case, we have some sympathy for him.

Go into your local store and you are inevitably immersed in streams of "muzak" flowing down the aisles; go out into the street and you are deafened by the roar of traffic; seek solace out in the countryside and somebody's radio invades your private world or a Boeing 707 roars overhead; turn on your TV to watch a favourite programme and a thunderous surge of so-called background music obliterates the things you really want to hear; enter some churches and it seems that, apart from an interlude called the sermon, the musicians are hardly ever silent (it would be less distracting if they softly played a recognisable melody instead of indeterminate trills). Perhaps that's why Matt Redman wrote his insightful song *When the Music Fades*, with its thought-provoking lines, "I'll bring you more than a song, for a song is not what you have required... I'm coming back to the heart of worship, and it's all about you, Jesus".

As a small boy with an over-active imagination, I overcame my fear of going upstairs at night-time by stamping on the stairs and singing or whistling loudly in the belief that this noisy display would warn whatever dark thing lurked upstairs that I was not afraid. In later life,

I had to put away this childish notion and understand that real power is not measured in decibels, that loudness cannot hide weakness, and that, very often, "empty vessels make most noise".

Against the background of a world in geophysical and political upheaval, Psalm 46 called for silence, *"Be still, and know that I am God"* (v 10). Like Elijah on Mount Horeb (1 Kings 19:11, 12), we eventually discover that the presence of God is often revealed not in impressive supernatural manifestations but in a low whisper heard only by a humble, listening ear.

Maybe we are afraid of silence because we don't know how to handle it. We fail to distinguish between stillness and deadness, and so, like Peter on the Mount of Transfiguration (Mark 9:5-8), feel we must always say something or do something to make the occasion meaningful, when God is actually calling us to turn our eyes upon Jesus and listen to him.

It would, of course, be foolish to argue that the presence of God is made known only in times of quietness. The Scriptures are full of exhortations to praise the Lord with songs and shouts of praise, trumpets and *"loud sounding cymbals",* but maybe we have sometimes over-emphasised the latter and given ourselves concussion from too much percussion. We need to get the balance right.

Christmas presents us with a typical dilemma: is it to be *Silent Night* or *Hark! The Herald Angels Sing*? Our answer is likely to be a matter of personal music taste rather than theology, and, just as likely, due to the mood of the moment, but that's to be on dangerous ground. The truth is, they're different sides of the same coin and how it falls depends very much, in more senses than one, on how you spin it.

## If You Want to Celebrate Christmas, Wear a Tin Hat!

**D**ressed as Eastern shepherds, a group of men stood, somewhat self-consciously, round the crib where a doll lay amid the straw. They were taking part in Cardiff City Temple choir's nativity play, part of its annual Christmas programme. All was going according to the script, until, suddenly, the "doll" moved! The shepherds, choir and congregation were stunned – there was real life in the manger!

It was only afterwards that the secret was disclosed: someone had replaced the doll with a living baby. But that's the truth about Christmas. God doesn't keep to our script. He replaces our easily manageable "dolls" with shocking reality; the conquering hero of Jewish messianic dreams slips unobtrusively into the world as a village girl's baby, his royal palace is the stable of a Bethlehem inn – but there's life in the manger!

Too often our ideas about Christmas are bland and sentimental – the "little Lord Jesus" who, according to the carol, doesn't cry; the "silent night" where "all is calm, all is bright"; the trio of exotic kings and their shiny gifts; the air-brushed pictures of the cleanest animals that ever inhabited a stable. Moist-eyed parents watch little Wayne and Jemima in school nativity plays, record shops are awash with the latest seasonal celebrity discs, and hard-nosed business executives send "appropriate" cards adorned with Old Masters' versions of the nativity. So long as Jesus is left in the manger, so long as he doesn't move, everyone is happy to celebrate Christmas.

The trouble is – he does move! The "little Lord Jesus" grows up and begins to move down country lanes and city streets, on storm-tossed seas and lonely deserts. And he does cry – weeping with bereaved sisters at a brother's grave, weeping over a doomed city that had rejected him, weeping great gut-wrenching sobs as he wrestles with demonic powers in the darkness of Gethsemane. There's not much calm where Jesus is.

Incarnation is not just a pretty story; it means labour pains, blood and tears, disturbed nights with a crying baby, the anxieties of parenting, the struggles of teenage years and manhood, the cost of sacrificial ministry, the trauma of the cross. It is not only singing angels and worshipping wise men, it is also Herod's savage sword dripping with baby blood.

The truth is that Christmas is not so much a day for party hats as for tin hats. It is "D-Day", when God invades planet earth in order to *"destroy him who holds the power of death – that is, the devil – and free those who all their lives were held in slavery by their fear of death"* (Hebrews 2:14, 15).

Bethlehem is more than a birthplace, it is a bridgehead – the place where the liberating Christ begins his march to final conquest. It is the place where the despotic ambitions of Herod, and, behind him, all the high command of hell's warlords, are "vexed to nightmare by a rocking cradle".

The real Jesus is not a manageable doll that can be put away with the rest of the Christmas trivia until next year; he is the living Christ of God who comes into the world as prophet, priest and king. He declares the truth God commands us to hear, he is the mediator who alone can bring us into meaningful relationship with God, and he comes to establish God's final authority over people and nations.

The Christ of Bethlehem summons us to acknowledge his Lordship, accept his saving power, and follow him as he goes forth to wage war on the hosts of darkness and establish the Kingdom of God. Incarnation means invasion; it is a war on error, and it calls for more than celebration; it calls for consecration and commitment. Party if you will, but be prepared to follow the King as he leads his church against the gates of hell. You'll need a tin hat for that!

## *You Should Have Seen His face*

**Y**ou should have seen it! The look on his face. They were all in the church, you see, and there was this big argument going on. There was this chap who had been healed – no doubt about it! I mean, we all knew him. Been there for years he had. He'd got this shriveled hand – you could see it, all twisted up it was. Nobody ever felt like touching it.

Well, as I say, Jesus comes into this service this particular day and goes and heals him – just like that! I mean, it was terrific. But what actually happened was, he asked the man to stand up in front of everyone, and then he says, challenging like, *"Which is lawful on the Sabbath: to do good, or to do evil, to save life or to kill?"*

Well, nobody said a word. You could cut the atmosphere with a knife. It was like a graveyard, it was so silent.

But you should have seen his face! He was white with anger. His eyes flashed like torches of fire and his gaze swept over everyone in the building like a searchlight. Then he called the man to him and told him to stretch out his hand and there it was, perfectly healed.

I didn't know he could be angry like that. Mark said it was because of *"their stubborn hearts"* (Mark 3:5), because, I suppose, they put religious traditions, rules and regulations before the needs of the people. I didn't think he'd get so upset over something like that. He must care about people's needs much more than we seem to do. We seem to be so concerned with organisation, structures, methods, statistics, etc, but he just seems concerned about people.

...............................................................................................................

I can't say I took to him really. He was kind of a Yuppie – you know, a young chap with plenty of money, but mean with it, who held down a pretty good job – and had a very good opinion of himself, too. No, he wasn't my type at all. In fact, if I'm honest, he got on my nerves.

There he stood asking these pious questions about eternal life – and claiming to have kept all ten commandments – and I thought to myself, "Why does Jesus bother with filthy rich people like him?"

Then I looked at Jesus – and, well, you should have seen his face! He stood there looking at this young fellow and instead of fixing him with a stern, disapproving gaze, you could see, as Mark said later, that *"Jesus looking at him, loved him"* Mark 10:21. It was written all over his face! You know, it wasn't some soft, sentimental expression, but there was a gentleness – a kind of understanding, compassionate look. To be honest, I don't quite know how to describe it, but you could see that he loved him.

Sometimes I don't know quite what to make of Jesus. He seems to love the people everyone else loves to hate. I mean, look at some of his disciples – I really can't think what he sees in them, but he goes on loving them. Of course, we're not all like that, some of us are… well, different…

..........................................................................................................

I couldn't believe it! There we were, everybody cheering and as happy as could be. It was a beautiful spring morning, and from the hillside the city looked a picture, its honey coloured walls and battlemented towers glowing in the morning sun. You could see the great temple towering majestically above all the clustered houses and palaces, and I found myself humming Psalm 48. You know, the one that goes, *"Beautiful for situation, the joy of the whole earth, is Mount Zion…"*

Suddenly everything came to a halt. Jesus got off the donkey and stood staring at the city below. You should have seen his face! It was full of pain and he was crying! First of all, I thought it must be that he was moved by the sheer beauty of the city, but then he began to speak and I realized he was crying for another reason.

Later on, Luke mentioned it in his account of what happened: he said, *"As he drew near, he saw the city and wept over it…"* (19:41). What was all the more surprising to me was what Jesus was saying. I mean

55

he was talking about the judgement that would fall on the city because it had rejected him, but he was crying as he spoke. He wasn't angry this time, just incredibly sad.

If it had been me, I would have felt, "serve them right for not listening to me!" But not him, he cried. They tell me he cried at Lazarus' tomb, even though he knew he was going to raise him from the dead. I suppose he was just moved to tears by the sight of Mary and Martha weeping. He seems to be so tenderhearted.

..................................................................................

It was Luke who told us about it afterwards. I'm not sure how he got to know, but someone who was there must have told him – unless it was Peter himself. Anyway, they arrested Jesus and took him to Caiaphas' palace for interrogation. Peter had run away when things started to hot up in the Garden of Gethsemane, but then he decided to follow the crowd to see what would happen.

He managed to get inside the palace courtyard and was warming himself by the fire – it was quite a cold night, you see. Well, this girl accused him of being a follower of Jesus, but he denied it. Then a couple of other people said the same thing, and Peter got really uptight. He stood there in the firelight swearing and cursing and saying he didn't know Jesus. And just at that moment a cock started crowing somewhere or other.

Whether or not Jesus heard, I don't know, but he was not far away, because Luke said that, as Peter blurted out the words, *"the Lord turned and looked at Peter"* (22:61). You should have seen the look on Jesus face! It wasn't anger, nor even the "I told you so" look that some people give when other people haven't lived up to their promises. Of course, Peter had said he would never let Jesus down, and Jesus had warned him that before the cock crowed he would deny him three times.

It's difficult to describe that look. It seemed to be full of mingled pity, disappointment, anguish, love and forgiveness. But really it was beyond description. Peter could hardly bear to look at Jesus, but he remembered what Jesus had said to him, and he turned and blundered out into the darkness and cried and cried… He could never forget that look.

. . . . . . . . . . . . . . . . . . . . . . . . . . . . . . . . . . . . . . . . . . . . . . . . . . . . . . . . . . . . . . . . . . . . . . . .

Did you ever see that photograph of King George V talking to a little boy? The king had his back to the camera, but you could tell he had a kind face, even though you couldn't see it, because of the expression on the little boy's face. The lad was smiling so happily and trustingly as he looked up at the king that his face mirrored the kindness of the king's. I suppose it's a bit like that with Jesus. You look at the people who met him and see the reflection of his glory in them – except for once.

I was going to say, "You should have seen his face!" But it doesn't seem right to say it this time. Nobody really knows what he actually looked like, but I can't help feeling he did have a lovely face. There were certainly no "worry lines", no marks of sin and no furtive looks. In fact like Psalm 45:2 says, he was *"fairer than all the sons of men"*. He was the *"altogether lovely one."* That was, until the vandals went to work on him. After that, as Isaiah said, *"His appearance was so disfigured beyond that of any man"* (52:14 NIV).

It was awful. They hit him, spat into his face, beat him, crowned him with thorns, tortured him until his face was contorted with agony…

Perhaps the hymn puts it more appropriately:

> *Extended on a cursed tree,*
> *Besmeared with dust, and sweat, and blood,*
> *See there, the King of Glory see!*
> *Sinks and expires the Son of God.*

You hardly dare think about it.

. . . . . . . . . . . . . . . . . . . .   . . . . . . . . . . . . . . . . . . . . . . . . . . . . . . . . . . . . . . . . . . . . . . . . . . . . .

It was a Sunday. John was an old man by now – about 90, I believe. It seems the Romans were getting tough with the Church and had arrested him and carted him off to this prison island. Anyhow, he was having a time of prayer somewhere in the camp (marvelous how those old Christians kept seeking the Lord wherever they were!) and suddenly Jesus stood there before him!

Well, you should have see Jesus' face! John said it was like the sun at its noonday full strength. His eyes were like a flame of fire and out of his mouth flashed a two edged sword (Revelation 1:16). It was absolutely awe-inspiring. In fact, John said it was so full of majesty and power that he fell down trembling in fear. But then the Lord spoke to him and told him that he had risen from the dead and now held the keys of human destiny in his hands.

Actually, Peter, James and John had seen something of that glory once before – when Jesus was transfigured – and Saul of tarsus had seen it too – when he was on the road to Damascus to kill the Christians. In fact, he said it was *"brighter than the sun."*

I don't know whether that was in his mind when he wrote the words, perhaps not, but when he wrote his second letter to the church at Corinth, Paul talked about seeing *"the glory of God in the face of Christ."*

Anyway, it started me thinking about the face of Jesus and the people who had seen it when he was on earth. That man, whoever he was, who wrote the letter to the Hebrews said that Jesus was the *"exact likeness of God,"* the "living image", you might say. Come to think of it, Jesus himself said, *"He who has seen me has seen the father,"* John 14:9.

In that case, the glory of God in the face of Jesus Christ was like one of those kaleidoscope things – you know, full of changing colours: anger, love, compassion, pity, sorrow, suffering, untold beauty and glory. And when you think about the things that made him angry, the people whom he loved and had compassion on, they way they treated him – and the glory that shone out in the darkness of the world, you begin to feel you've seen something of what God is really like. And you can't help feeling that he really is wonderful!

## Don't Leave Jesus in the Back Seat!

They were fishermen and he was a carpenter by trade. They were setting out to sea, so they knew they could leave him in the back seat. After all, this was their scene. They had been sailing these waters for years and knew them like the backs of their hands. They were in their element. So, Mark tells us, *"they took him"* (Mark 1:36).

This was one place where he wasn't needed – until the storm! That taught them that there was no area of life – even the ones where their expertise had been honed to its sharpest – where they could afford to attempt anything without his empowering presence. Only by restoring him to the centre of the situation was there any hope of success.

Two newspaper reports have reminded me of that story. One was an account of a conversation with Dr Rowan Williams the Archbishop of Canterbury entitled, *Explaining God to the Godless*, in which he was asked a series of philosophical questions about the existence and nature of God. Granted the questions required a certain academic response, but one striking omission caused head-shaking astonishment: the head of a worldwide Christian Church sought to explain God to the godless without a single reference to the Lord Jesus Christ! Jesus was left in the theological back seat.

The other report was equally disturbing: "Churches 'on road to doom' if trends continue." A report by the Christian Research organisation predicts that, "by 2040 there will be nearly twice as many Muslims at prayer in mosques on Friday as Christians worshipping in church on Sundays." The report predicts "a demoralised Church of England struggling against the forces of secularism", faith schools becoming multi-faith schools, *Songs of Praise* being taken off the air, Alpha courses being abandoned and Christmas rebranded as "Winterval". The picture is stark.

The conclusions of that research may be wildly pessimistic, but they should at least shake any complacency we might have. The striking thing for me is what seems a significant connection between these reports. They seem to underline an inescapable conclusion. When Jesus is no longer central to the Church's theology, when he is left in the back seat while a self-sufficient Church relies on her own expertise to meet the challenge of the contemporary world, when the Church worships him as Lord and then proceeds to ignore him in the day-to-day practicalities of personal and congregational life, when prayerlessness and the general decline in reading and obeying the Scriptures are the hallmark of much that passes for modern spirituality, when worship is self-centred, when "church" means pleasing people rather than exalting Christ, when our bright ideas replace the direction of the Holy Spirit, and when Christians commit adultery with the world, then Christ is left in the back seat and the Church will face the inevitable storm without him. Unless it repents.

Christ-centredness was the hallmark of the early Church. He stood astride the landscape of their thinking like a colossus, towering above everything else. Paul might quote pagan poets in his encounter with the philosophers, but he moved inevitably to the truth about Jesus (Acts 17:31). To the first Christians, Jesus was not merely a kindly teacher who walked about the shores of Galilee wearing sandals, telling lovely stories. To them he was *"both Lord and Christ"* (Acts 2:36), the *"Author of life"* (Acts 3:14), the only name by which men may be saved (Acts 4:12), a *"Prince and a Saviour"* (Acts 5:31), the *"Son of Man"* (Acts 7:56), the one *"appointed by God to be judge of the living and the dead"* (Acts 10:42), and *"Head over everything for the Church, which is his body..."* (Ephesians 1:21, 22).

Jesus Christ was the focus of their worship, the subject of their message, the centre of their fellowship and the object of their passionate love. Everything revolved around him. No political or religious correctness watered down the unequivocal message and lifestyle of this Church to which God added multitudes of converts. They overcame the storms of opposition and persecution that raged against them because Jesus Christ was never in the back seat. He was always up front. That's a lesson the modern Church must learn.

## What Jesus Taught about Signs and Wonders

Miracles have always created controversy. In Jesus' day there were furious arguments over his own ministry, some attributing his miracles to the devil and others welcoming them as indisputable evidence of his divinity (John 9:33; cf. 10:19-21). The debate has reverberated through the centuries and still rumbles on.

Jesus called for righteous judgment. In response to those who criticised him for breaking the boundaries of orthodox religion he said, *"Stop judging by appearances and make a right judgment"* (John 7:24). A glance at the men and women God has blessed and used over the centuries will reveal marked differences of personality, style, mode of dress and methods of ministry, and will prevent us from making superficial judgments on such grounds. Mark 9:38-40 reminds us that Jesus was sometimes far less fazed by "unauthorised" ministries than his trigger-happy followers were – and still are!

We cannot limit God to the narrow parameters of our preconceived ideas, prejudices or preferences. He is free to "do his own thing" (Numbers 11:16-29; Acts 10:14f.). Having said that, it is also clear that Jesus did not view signs and wonders ministry of itself as the guarantee of spiritual credibility. He certainly appealed to his own works as proofs of his divinity and as signs of the coming of the Kingdom of God (Luke 11:20; John 5:36), and commissioned his disciples to continue that ministry (Luke 10:9); but in a deeply disturbing passage he declared that it is possible to make correct Christological statements – to call him Lord and perform miracles in his name – and yet be exposed as a fraud at the day of judgment (Matthew 7:21-23). Like the sons of Sceva (Acts 19:13-17), it is possible to say *"In the name of Jesus"* as a kind of formula in performing miracles, and like Apollos (Acts 18:24-28), it is also possible to make accurate statements about him without fully *"preaching the truth as it is in Jesus"* (Ephesians 4:21). "Preaching Christ" is the declaration of his absolute supremacy as the Son of

God, the Saviour of men and Lord of all, the One before whom all people must kneel in repentance and faith.

Jesus saw miracles as supportive of, but secondary to, the preaching of the Gospel. He seems to say that faith based on signs and wonders is in some way inferior to faith in his word (John 10:37; 14:11). Unlike many contemporary ministries, on at least five occasions he sought to avoid publicity for his miracles (Matthew 9:30; 12:15-21; Mark 5:43; 7:36; 8:26). He certainly pointed to signs and wonders as evidence of the Kingdom (Matthew 11:2-5) but only in conjunction with preaching of the Word of God and its unequivocal demand for repentance (Matthew 4:17,23; Mark 1:14,15; Luke 4:16-21; 13:3). Apart from any observable signs, the Kingdom was already present (Luke 17:20, 21).

In the last analysis, miracles, for Jesus, were more than the supreme hallmark of God's approval on his life and ministry, and certainly more than impressive displays of power. Matthew (12:15-21) quotes Isaiah in painting a picture of the unpretentious Saviour graciously and unassumingly reaching out a loving hand to touch and restore broken people. He was *"moved with compassion"*.

Like motorway signs, the miracles pointed to realities beyond themselves. Merely being taken up with them as exciting demonstrations of power and enjoying their physical benefits was to miss their true meaning and fail to complete the journey of faith (John 6:26, 27; Mark 6:51, 52).

In the end, it was the preaching of the Gospel with its demand for repentance that Jesus insisted on. And it is that message which, above all other good but secondary issues, our godless and doomed generation needs to hear. From the blighted ghettos of hooded young street gangs to the luxurious apartments of prosperous sinners, our age needs to face the radical call to repentance and faith. That, supremely, is the evidence of the Holy Spirit at work, and the unmistakable sign of authentic revival (John 16:8-11).

## *Popcorn and the Passion*

The big screen flickered with fearful images of suffering as Roman whips criss-crossed the body of Christ with a savage tracery of torture, but the woman sat in her comfortable seat seemingly unmoved, clasping a huge tub of popcorn and munching away contentedly.

Maybe she was more moved than she seemed, perhaps the popcorn was a kind of confectioned anodyne against too much emotional distress. But, for whatever reason, she held on to her popcorn while she watched *The Passion of the Christ*.

Perhaps it was the kind of defence-mechanism we deploy when we are not too sure of how to cope with the unfamiliar – like the way we nervously want to giggle in otherwise solemn moments. Nonetheless, popcorn and *The Passion* seemed uneasy companions, even in the darkened anonymity of a cinema.

Someone once commented on the strangeness of the topics dark-suited men start to talk about within five minutes of seeing a coffin lowered into the ground. Hardly have the solemn words of the committal died on the wind before they reach for their cigarettes and start discussing stocks and shares or soccer, or the latest show they have been to see. We have an innate ability to turn the most serious moments of life into superficiality. Quickly loosening our ties and reaching for the next sausage roll, we dissolve eternity in a weak solution of triviality.

The popcorn mentality trivialises sin. Lies become "economy with the truth", adultery becomes "an affair", the killing of a baby in the womb becomes "the termination of a pregnancy", homosexuality becomes "being gay", and fraud and dishonesty become "playing the system". The list of euphemisms for sin is endless – but we must never forget that merely changing the name doesn't change the nature. Sin is *"the transgression of the law"* (1 John 3:4), it is rebellion against the holy God whose awesome but righteous anger against all forms of sin will result in final judgement (Romans 1:18f). The cross of Christ is itself an expression of that judgement – and only at the cross can men and women find salvation from the power and penalty of sin.

There is a distressing sub-plot to the story of the cross – the sight of Roman soldiers gambling for the clothes of Jesus. In their hard professionalism, they are heedless of the slow drip of his life's blood above them. They simply concentrate on getting something for themselves out of his suffering, and the click of the dice obliterates the cry of the crucified.

Yet Christians, too, sometimes play games at the foot of the cross! Some career-motivated people play ecclesiastical politics beneath the cross of Jesus, more concerned with exercising "leadership" in the local church or climbing denominational ladders than hearing the call of the crucified Lord to humble obedience. Others of us, especially preachers, singers and musicians, are tempted to "play to the gallery" – loving the applause of men rather than the approval of the thorn-crowned One. And many of us, perhaps most of us, spend a lot of our time and energy on working out the best options for ourselves. We don't actually gamble on the seamless robe, but we're more concerned with the blessings we can get from him than with the claims he makes upon us.

It is easy to sing, "Love so amazing, so divine, demands my soul, my life, my all", but if we are honest, there are many other things that make demands upon our time and enthusiasm and commitment. Too often we play the game of Trivial Pursuit while a godless world rages against the cross and the crucified Lord looks down upon our preoccupation with our private concerns. The serpent, who subtly appealed to our first parents' self interest and proud ambition in Eden, still lurks on the slopes of Calvary. We are still tempted to play Snakes and Ladders at the foot of the cross.

"Popcorn Christianity" is sweet-toothed. It "surveys the wondrous cross" through a soft-focus lens. It does not wish to hear the crack of the whips or the dull thud of the hammers, and recoils from the harshness of all the sounds of crucifixion. It rejoices in the final cry, *"It is finished!"* but hesitates over being *"crucified with Christ"*. It craves *"the power of his resurrection"*, but declines *"the fellowship of his sufferings"* (Philippians 3:10). It makes the cross a logo, but not a lifestyle.

When you come to think about it, popcorn and *The Passion* don't really look right together – do they?

## There is no Ring Road Round Calvary

The TV presenter Sally Magnusson tells an intriguing story in her book *Glorious Things* about an encounter between the former Poet Laureate, John Betjeman, and a brash young man who was interviewing him on a TV programme. In a dismissive tone of voice the young man referred to hymns as "worthless doggerel".

Betjeman paused for a moment and then quietly said, "Ah, I see what you mean," and went on to quote the lines,

> *His dying crimson, like a robe,*
> *Spreads o'er His body on the tree;*
> *Then am I dead to all the globe,*
> *And all the globe is dead to me.*

The young man was silenced – and shamed.

The words Betjeman quoted are from a verse – sadly, almost always omitted from hymnbooks and hardly ever sung – from Isaac Watts' magnificent hymn, *When I Survey The Wondrous Cross*.

Vividly and movingly, they remind us of the horror and the power of the cross of Calvary and prepare us for the challenge of the final verse of the hymn: *Love so amazing, so divine, demands... my all.*

It is not likely that any real Christians would treat such a hymn as doggerel, though some might treat it – as they do most hymns – as a museum piece; but the danger is that while we enjoy its poetry we evade its theology.

Like the apostle Paul, Isaac Watts knew that the cross of Christ "towering o'er the wrecks of time" – to quote yet another "redundant" hymn – is the final challenge to human pride and self-centredness. The cross reduces all our claims to superiority, whether they are ethnic, social, religious, intellectual, theological, professional, or of any other kind, to a humiliating heap of sin-damaged tawdriness.

The cross of Christ is the focal point at which three roads converge: it is the place where the exceeding sinfulness of sin, the awesome justice of God and God's amazing grace meet in dynamic encounter.

The cross shows up in stark relief the truth about the world. It strips away the masks of religious pretence, political expediency and popular morality, and reveals the unacceptable face of human corruption. What men did at Calvary reveals what sin is and what it does.

The cross reveals the ultimate verdict of a holy God upon sin. Modern theologians, even some evangelical ones, want to soften the truth about the wrath of God, but Jesus had no such hesitation. Approaching his death he cried, *"Now is the time for judgment of this world; now the prince of this world will be driven out"* (John 12:31).

The horrific nature of sin and the awesome nature of God were in collision at Calvary. Sin is lawlessness (1 John 3:4); therefore *"the Judge of all the earth"* must deal with it, otherwise moral anarchy will destroy the universe. Jesus understood that.

But the cross is also the ultimate revelation of God's grace: *"He saw that there was no man, and wondered that there was no one to intercede; then his own arm brought him salvation, and his righteousness upheld him"* (Isaiah 59:16, ESV). *"God shows his love for us in that while we were still sinners, Christ died for us"* (Romans 5:8, ESV).

Calvary is the place where "heaven's love and heaven's justice meet". The outstretched arms of the Crucified offer the mercy of a holy God.

It is against the background of Calvary that Paul's great affirmation in Galatians 6:20 and Isaac Watts' echoing hymn resonate. To "survey the wondrous cross" is to renounce the world that put him there; to have nothing to do with its smiling hypocrisies; to reject its soiled values; to spurn its enticements; and to refuse to compromise with its rejection of God.

The cross deals a death blow to my aspirations to "get on" in the world that crucified – and still rejects – my Lord and Saviour; but it also calls me to share his passion for the lost and to proclaim the good news of his grace.

That's why there is no ring road round Calvary – it is the unavoidable crossroads of human destiny.

# Slow Down!
# You are now Approaching Gethsemane

Like some of those ancient buildings that escaped Henry VIII's dissolution of the monasteries in the sixteenth century and still stand to the glory of God, there are some old hymns that have survived the dissolution of the hymnbooks in the mid twentieth century and are still occasionally sung. Among them is number 176 in the *Redemption Hymnal* – *"I stand amazed in the presence of Jesus the Nazarene"*. It has a problem, though: the marriage of words and tune is not an entirely happy one. The lively tune has a built-in accelerator that causes it to be sung at times with ever-increasing speed.

The theme of the hymn is Christ's wonderful love for us revealed in Gethsemane and the Cross; but singing it in a meeting some time ago we found ourselves driving through Gethsemane and round Calvary at 80 miles an hour, with little time to ponder the fact that in the garden "He had no tears for His own griefs, but sweat drops of blood for mine", or to "survey the wondrous cross". We had broken the Gethsemane speed limit! We didn't mean to be thoughtless or irreverent, but the tune had taken over. We were going too fast to take in the view.

That incident highlights some important issues for Christians living in a world in which time and motion determine the pace of life. It reminds us of those subtle but highly significant shifts of priority which influence our spiritual life. For instance, it reveals how remarkably easy it is for the secondary (the tune) to dominate the primary (the words) and in so doing alter the nature and quality of an act of worship. Sometimes the music takes precedence over the message, and if we are not careful, instead of pondering and evaluating the implications of the truth (and sometimes the untruth) of what we are singing, we are simply taken up with the undoubted pleasure of engaging in corporate worship. We need to remember that it is the truth, not the tune, that sets us free (John 8:32, 33).

In the same way, working for God sometimes takes precedence over knowing God. Like the boy Samuel (1 Samuel 3:1-7), it is possible to live in a religious environment and to exercise regular service in the house of God and yet not know the Lord (v.7). As Jesus reminded Martha (Luke 10:38-41), there are times when serving God becomes more important to us than sitting at his feet and listening to him in humble submission to his Word. Like Martha, we become *"distracted with much serving"*, and sometimes highly critical of those who do not share our enthusiastic activism. But as Jesus said, we need to get our priorities right: *"You are worried and upset about many things, but only one thing is needed"* (vv. 41, 42). Of course, energetic service for God is vital; but it must be based on a deep relationship with him and continuing exposure to all that he is in himself and his Word. As Paul put it when considering his own outstanding track record: *"I consider everything a loss compared to the surpassing greatness of knowing Christ Jesus my Lord... I want to know Christ and the power of his resurrection and the fellowship of sharing in his sufferings"* (Philippians 3:8, 10). Serving God must come second to knowing him, working for him second to walking with him.

Gethsemane and Calvary demand that we slow down and examine our personal priorities. In an age where, in both the secular and spiritual realms, success is measured by the attainment of universally applauded goals and the achievement of personal ambitions, and where we are offered fast-track routes to celebrity status, we need to face the question: is it my success or God's glory that really motivates me? We need to listen to the voice of John the Baptist: *"He must become greater; I must become less"*(John 5:30); and the words of Paul: *"May I never boast except in the cross of our Lord Jesus Christ"* (Galatians 6:14). Supremely, we need to ponder the words of Jesus himself on that dreaded Calvary road: *"Now my heart is troubled, and what shall I say? 'Father, save me from this hour'? No... Father, glorify your name!"* (John 12:27, 28). We need the Gethsemane speed limit not to curb our enthusiasm, but to help us to see where we're going – in more senses than one!

## *Kohima and Calvary*

High in the hills of Assam the small town of Kohima was the scene of the final World War II battle that decided the fate of India. A seemingly all-victorious Japanese army was poised for the conquest of the great sub-continent, and only the battered troops of the British Fourteenth Army stood against them. So intense was the battle that at one time the two armies faced each other from opposite ends of the Assistant Commissioner's tennis court! Finally, after fearful suffering and loss, the defenders held out and India was saved.

Our RAF convoy drove into Kohima some time later, and the scene of utter desolation is etched on my memory forever. The mountain road wound its way among fire-blasted hills strewn with the debris of war. Scattered groups of stunted trees, their branches savagely pruned by high explosives, stood on the hillsides like black crosses gaunt against the sky.

Kohima was an awful place, desolate and ruined, where men fought and died, where hatred and fear joined hands, where guns thundered and shells screamed, where the earth itself was scarred by steel and stained by human blood. But it was also the place of a decisive victory.

Now, when I remember Kohima, I am moved to think of Calvary, where the Saviour of the world kept what Alan Seeger called, "a rendezvous with death... on some scarred slope of battered hill," and fought the great, decisive battle against the hosts of hell. To me, those gaunt trees still stand as symbols of "a tree as bare as the winds of winter could make it – the great, grim, dear, wondrous cross of Christ," as Joseph Parker movingly described it.

Calvary was an awful place, where the hosts of hell massed against one lonely human being who was also God incarnate, where a deadly coalition of corrupt politics, fanatical religion and fickle public opinion hounded Jesus to death. It was a place of blood and blasphemy, of agony and infamy, a place where sin finally shook its rebellious fist in the face of a Creator God, and whipped and nailed his only Son to death. But it was also the place where "love so amazing" won the final victory.

Today, a memorial to those who died at Kohima stands there bearing this inscription: "When you go home, tell them that for your tomorrow we gave our today". It is a call for reflection and thanksgiving, and it is also a challenge to the thoughtless hedonism of a generation that forgets that its freedom was only won at a fearful cost. It echoes a call we need to hear afresh amid our preoccupation with lesser things.

In the annual Festival of Remembrance in the Royal Albert Hall, the most moving moment comes when the marching up and down ceases and the spectacular displays come to an end. Then the bands stop playing and, in the silence, millions of poppy petals cascade from the dome in a blood-red rain of remembrance. It is only then that the real meaning of war is made known.

In the same way the Church needs to pause amid its preoccupation with secondary things – developing structures, launching programmes, perfecting worship styles, studying the latest models of "doing church", marching up and down in restless activity and ceaseless sound, pursuing personal agendas – and face afresh the challenge of the cross of Christ.

We need to stop "doing church" in the usual way and pause long enough to actually hear what the Father said when Peter wanted to "erect structures" on the mountain (Matthew 17:1-5): *This is my beloved Son... Listen to him.* After all, it was for our eternal "tomorrow" that he gave his earthly "yesterday". He deserves much more of our attention than we usually give him.

## *Discovering the Treasures of the Tomb*

On November 26, 1922, Lord Carnarvon stood impatiently outside the tomb of Tutankhamen in the sun-drenched Valley of the Kings in Egypt while his friend, the archaeologist Howard Carter, sought to find entrance into the hitherto unexplored royal burial place.

Howard Carter tells the story of that momentous day: "Presently, as my eyes grew accustomed to the light, details of the room within emerged slowly from the mist, strange animals, statues and gold – everywhere the glint of gold," he wrote. "When Lord Carnarvon, unable to stand the suspense any longer, enquired anxiously, 'Can you see anything?' It was all I could do get out the words, 'Yes, wonderful things!'".

Some of those "wonderful things" when on display in London have drawn huge crowds of people to gaze at the treasures found in the boy king's tomb; but there is another royal tomb that contains even more wonderful things. True, there are no gilded artifacts to be found in this tomb, only an abandoned shroud; yet everywhere there is the glint of gold – not the gold of earthly values but the shining glory of an astonishing triumph over death. And although the exact location of that tomb is no longer known, the truth it enshrines is eternal.

The words *"that he was buried"* (1 Corinthians 15:4) seem almost to break the flow of Paul's thought, but they are important because they state the fact that he who came to die to save us from our sins actually did so. The tomb in Joseph's garden, sealed and guarded by the state (Matthew 27:62-66), is a "death certificate" carved in stone confirming the fact that Jesus went all the way to save us.

To the casual visitor, the tomb of Jesus, unlike the panoplied tombs of earthly kings, held nothing worth looking at, only discarded grave clothes; but when John gave them a second, more careful look they assumed a breath-taking, faith-creating significance (John 20:3-8). The fact that they remained completely intact as a tightly wound shroud yet contained no body made him realise that the body they had enclosed had passed through them in an act of mysterious life and awesome power. He knew that something had happened in this tomb which would change the course of history and profoundly affect his personal life.

Like a standard lowered in defeat, those discarded grave clothes announced the fact that Satan, sin and death had succumbed to the power of the risen Christ. Paul's words, *"But now is Christ risen from the dead"* (1 Corinthians 15:20) are like a trumpet call sounding through the smoke of battle in a thrilling declaration of his victory in the crucial battle of Calvary. "Death could not keep its prey, He tore its bars away", and in the immaculate splendour of his sinless life he rose triumphantly.

The empty tomb is flooded with the light of resurrection morning and echoes to the voice of the Spirit declaring that the crucified Jesus is truly the Son of God (Romans 1:4), the Saviour of men (1 Corinthians 15:17-22), and Lord of the world's destiny (Acts 2:32-36). The showy trinkets of earthly power are missing in this tomb, but, symbolically, everywhere there is the glint of gold, and spiritually enlightened eyes are entranced by the sight of the wonderful things which lie beyond its open door.

And by the way, that stone the state sealed and set its soldiers to guard was found rolled away with its seal snapped, its guard immobilised, and an angel nonchalantly sitting on it – a somewhat bizarre reminder of the fact that, placed in the context of the glory of the risen Christ, all human claims to authority, whether secular or religious, are ultimately rather pompous and certainly ridiculous. Facing the truth of the resurrection, the only reasonable response is to kneel with doubting Thomas, and humbly say, *"My Lord and my God."*

## Let's see the Power of Jesus' Resurrection in our Everyday Lives

Suppose you had been assigned the task of stage-managing the most remarkable event in history – the resurrection of Jesus Christ. How would you have done it, and where? With a gigantic Hollywood-style extravaganza in Rome, nerve centre of world politics? Or in Athens or Corinth, capitals of culture? Or in Jerusalem, whose glorious temple dominated the religious scene? What an opportunity to confront Caesar, the Greek philosophers, Caiaphas, Pilate, Herod and the motley rabble that shouted for Jesus' death with the breathtaking splendour of his triumph! Spin-doctors and showmen of the religious world unite!

But how does God do it?

In a cemetery, where a broken-hearted woman weeps. On a dusty road – where two people trudge into the sunset of all their hopes. In a locked upper room – where eleven men, gripped by fear, start at every creak of the stairs. On the shores of a lake – where seven men sit hunched over their oars becalmed on the grey waters of failure. On the main road to Damascus – where a man driven by hatred of Christ hurries on a mission of murder. On the lonely shores of Patmos, a Roman Guantanamo Bay-style prison camp – where an old man still seeks, in spite of the harsh regime, to be *"in the Spirit on the Lord's day"*.

The truth is that Jesus *"showed himself alive"* (Acts 1:3) not so much in big events, though there were some, as Acts 2 tells us, but in personal encounters and amid personal circumstances which remind us that Easter Day can happen any day and anywhere. We can experience the power of the Lord's resurrection not only in crowded celebrations or, for that matter, in meetings of any kind, though he has promised to be in the midst when we gather together in his name, but also in the ordinary situations of everyday life – in the kitchen, the classroom, the shopping mall, the hospital ward, the office, on the factory floor, or in the prison cell. The locations of resurrection reality are limitless!

The experience of the presence of the risen Christ will bring comfort when we sorrow, fresh perspectives on the Emmaus Road of our perplexity about the meaning of life, assurance when fear would imprison us behind the locked doors of our own inadequacies, and power into situations where we are numbed by an awareness of failure.

It will also confront our angry rebellion with grace and minister to our sense of isolation with the touch of an all-pervading presence. The fact of the resurrection tells not only of an historic event in which Satan was defeated, when sin was atoned for and death lost its sting, but also brings the limitless resources of the all-conquering Christ into daily life. As the poet sang,

*O Christians, who throng Holborn and Fifth Avenue,*
*May you not meet, in spite of death, a traveller from*
*Nazareth?*

Yet we can miss him in "life's throng and press" – unless, like John on Patmos (read Revelation 1:10-18 carefully), we seek daily to be *"in the Spirit"*, and *"hear"* (listen for) his voice, *"turn to see"* (respond to His call), *"see"* (make time to look at) his revelation of himself, and *"fall at his feet"* in worship (if not physically, always, at least in spirit). Only then we shall know an encounter with the risen One. But it can happen anytime and anywhere. Expect him to come and look out for him today!

## *Loose the Grave Clothes!*

There was a time on Easter Sundays when churches resembled a Paris fashion show. New outfits were on proud display and hats blossomed everywhere like a millinery Kew Gardens. Even the men sported new ties. Easter seemed to be more sartorial than spiritual. Thankfully, that day has passed – but I am not sure that what has taken its place is any better.

There now seems to be a rather colourless conformity to the drab uniform of what the modern world calls "casual". Jeans-clad, T-shirted, tie-less, and often in non-descript woollies, many modern worshippers proclaim their freedom from tradition by a strange slavery to contemporary fashion.

I'm not quite sure what God makes of it all. Come to think of it, he has splashed colour everywhere in his creation and colour-coded the designs of his tabernacle and temple in red, blue, white, purple, gold, and the iridescent flash of precious stones. As Jesus said, God has robed the flowers of the field in colours and forms that put Solomon in all his glory in the shade.

It is true, of course, the Bible does tell us that outward appearance is not the most important thing — it's the state of the heart that matters. But that in itself is a reminder that, whatever we wear at Easter, we must not dumb down the message it proclaims. "The resurrection of Christ," said A.M.Hunter, is "the diamond pivot on which the whole truth of Christianity turns." To fail to respond to its magnificent implications is unthinkable. There is no place for a "casual" attitude to the truth of the Resurrection of Jesus Christ.

God help the Church when she trivializes the Easter message. God help the preachers who "chatter in Church like jackdaws" and waffle on about secondary issues and fail to proclaim Christ crucified and risen on Easter Day! God help the church members to whom Easter is mainly the first major holiday of the year — time to get out into the garden, spring clean the caravan, and go for country walks — and

God help the Christians who seem to think – Teletubby-like – more of cuddly bunnies, little lambs, fluffy chicks and chocolate eggs than they do of the Lord Christ risen from the dead.

The Easter message is in fact a fanfare proclaiming the deity of the Lord Jesus Christ: he is *"declared with power to be the Son of God by the resurrection from the dead"* (Romans 1:4). It is God saying with dramatic emphasis: *"This is my beloved Son in whom I am well pleased."* That is a call to worship.

The Easter message is a trumpet calling through the swirling smoke of battle proclaiming the victory of Christ: *"Now is Christ risen from the dead"* (1 Corinthians 15:20). The awesome coalition of religious, political and demonic powers that encircled the lonely figure on the cross have been utterly routed! Sin, Satan, death and hell have been put to flight. "If Christ be not risen," writes George Eldon Ladd, "redemptive history ends in the cul-de-sac of a Palestinian grave." But he has risen - *"in the power of an indestructible life"* (Hebrews 7:16)! "After Calvary," exclaims Professor James S. Stewart, "it can never be midnight again," and it is the dawn of Easter day that breaks the power of the prince of darkness and sets the prisoners free. It is a call to faith and commitment.

The Easter message is a solemn declaration that the destiny of the universe is in the nail-pierced hands of the crucified and risen Lord of life: *"God has set a day when he will judge the world with justice by the man he has appointed. He has given proof of this to all men by raising him from the dead"* (Acts 17:3). As J.S. Stewart puts it, "The resurrection was, and is, the sign of God's unshakable determination to make Christ Lord of all." It is a call to a glorious hope, but also to reverence and godly fear.

However you dress this Easter, don't dumb down its message. Make time to think it through and face its implications. The important question is not, "What shall I wear?" but, with Paul in Philippians 3:7-14, "How can I know more deeply the presence and power of the risen Lord and live to glorify his name?"

## *The Eagle has Landed*

On 20th July 1969 a cryptic message crackled over the airwaves into NASA's Houston control room announcing news of one of the most stupendous events in history. It was the voice of American astronaut "Buzz" Aldrin saying, "Houston. Tranquility Bay. The Eagle has landed!" It was confirmation that mankind had successfully completed a breathtaking journey into space and landed on the moon. Aldrin's voice was to be followed by that of Neil Armstrong's in a famous statement of human achievement, "That's one small step for man; one giant leap for mankind."

At 9am on a spring morning around AD30 another message, equally astonishing and of even greater significance, echoed across the streets of Jerusalem. One-hundred-and-twenty men and women began cryptically to speak in languages they had never learned, announcing the completion of another stunning journey of achievement – the arrival in heaven of Jesus Christ. The "heavenly Eagle" had landed! *"Exalted to the right hand of God,"* Jesus had, in Peter's words, *"poured out what you now see and hear"* (Acts 2:32, 33).

Probably because it always occurs on a Thursday, Ascension Day is rarely celebrated to the same degree as Easter or Pentecost, yet it is an event of mind-blowing proportions and stupendous spiritual implications. What took years of scientific research and millions of dollars spent on an elaborate engineering project to lift the Apollo 11 rocket into space, God had eclipsed long before – calmly and effortlessly – when he raised Jesus to his right hand in the heavenlies. This gravity-defying miracle was a breathtaking manifestation of God's total control over his universe. No wonder the disciples stood *"gazing up into heaven"* (Acts 1:10, 11). They were gobsmacked!

But the Ascension was more than an experiment in celestial astronautics; it was the triumphant conclusion of an expedition into time and space by God's only Son on a mission to save the human race from final judgement. It was not merely the conquest of gravity; it was the triumph of grace. It was the conclusion of the supreme "Operation Overlord" – an invasion of liberation in which Jesus Christ rescued planet earth from destruction. The Ascension declared that Christ truly was the Son of God; it affirmed that in his death and resurrection he had broken the stranglehold of Satan's sinister empire, and, exalted to the right hand of God, he was "Lord of all being, throned afar".

The day of Pentecost consists of far more than spectacular phenomena – wind, fire and tongues – it is the proclamation of the exalted glory and enthronement of Christ. Pentecost means more than a baptism of power, the blossoming of spiritual fruit, or the bestowal of supernatural gifts; it is supremely the broadcast on a global wavelength announcing the victory and saving power of the risen Christ. Speaking in tongues is a cryptic message declaring that Jesus is back in his rightful place, and it is also an invitation to sinners to take one small step of faith which will result in a giant leap of heavenly joy in the fullness of his saving grace.

Ascension Day and Pentecost are inextricably linked. Pentecostal/charismatic spirituality must be more than the exploration of the supernatural for its own sake. It must be an ever-deepening expression of the lordship of Christ. Our corporate worship, our fellowship, our personal life-style, our exercise of the gifts of the Spirit, and every aspect of our existence and behaviour must exalt Jesus Christ and declare to the watching world that he is *"both Lord and Christ"*, the One who alone is able to save to the uttermost, and the One to whom God has entrusted the destiny of the human race and who is coming again in power and glory. It was for this purpose that the day of Pentecost dawned (Acts 1:8).

The exaltation of Christ to the place of ultimate power as Lord and Saviour, and the Spirit-empowered proclamation of his reign by the Church – Ascension and Pentecost – are the essential components of authentic Christianity. Come on, let's celebrate!

# The Spirit and the Church

# *Reflections*

## *The Prelude to Pentecost*

He prayed – and the fire fell! Silhouetted against the Carmel skyline, his arms uplifted, he was an iconic symbol of prevailing prayer. Watched in sullen silence by the representatives of contemporary society – a corrupt political leader (Ahab), a group of aggressive pagan "lifestyle gurus" (Baal's prophets), and a crowd of morally and spiritually bankrupt people – Elijah restored the broken altar of Jehovah, proclaiming his absolute supremacy, his awesome holiness, and his amazing grace towards repentant sinners. And when he prayed, the fire of God fell on that rebuilt altar (1 Kings 18:30-38).

He prayed – and the glory came! He built a temple, carefully following Spirit-inspired instructions; he restored the scriptural order of worship and now stood, hands uplifted in passionate intercession, seeking the blessing of God. Then he knelt down in a growing intensity of prayer, his hands outstretched towards heaven, and *"as soon as Solomon had finished his prayer, fire came down from heaven...and the glory of the Lord filled the Lord's house"* (2 Chronicles 7:1,2).

He prayed – and the Dove descended! Drops of Jordan water glistened on his back in the sunlight as he rose from his baptism. Pristine in his sinless perfection, Jesus had no need of such a baptism of repentance, but in humble submission to his Father's will, he chose to identify himself in every way with sinners and so *"to fulfil all righteousness"* on our behalf (Matthew 3:15). And *"when Jesus also was baptised and was praying, the heavens were opened, and the Holy Spirit descended on him in bodily form like a dove"* (Luke 21:22 ESV).

They prayed – and the wind of God filled the house! They had done what Jesus told them to do – with one heart and mind they had devoted themselves to waiting upon God in fervent prayer, believing his promise (Acts 1:4-8) of giving them the enduement with power that would transform them into the advance guard of the church militant. They were not disappointed: *"suddenly there came from heaven a sound like a mighty rushing wind, and it filled the entire house... and divided tongues of fire rested on each one of them. And they were all filled with the Holy Spirit and began to speak with other tongues as the Spirit gave them utterance"* (Acts 2:1-5; and then turn to Acts 4:24-31).

Two men prayed – and the walls of racial discrimination fell! One was a Pentecostal pioneer, but still imprisoned within the walls of his traditional religious mindset. To Peter, Gentiles were outsiders; a gentile home was a no-go area – but he was praying on a rooftop in Joppa, and God spoke to him. Thirty miles away, in Caesarea, a Roman soldier felt himself held captive behind the walls of a Gentile exclusion zone – *"alienated from the commonwealth of Israel... having no hope and without God in the world"* (Ephesians 2:12) – but he too was praying, and likewise God spoke to him. Responding to the word of God and open to the Spirit of God, these two men became the spiritual electrodes between which the luminous flow of the electricity of the Holy Spirit arced, demolishing the walls of religious convention and uniting Jew and Gentile in a surge of liberating power. It was Pentecost all over again (read Acts 10 – the whole of it!).

Most of these stories concern special events, but the lessons behind them are universal. They all enshrine two vital spiritual principles: 1) when men and women respond in obedience to the will of God, and 2) begin to seek the face of God in *"fervent, effectual prayer"*, he answers them, for *"When you seek me with all your heart, I will be found by you, declares the Lord, and I will restore your fortunes..."* (Jeremiah 29:13, 14). Obedient faith and humble prayer are always the prelude to Pentecost. There are no alternatives.

## *The Holy Spirit Does Know Best!*

You're a worship leader. You and the group have prayed and practised for today. A small pile of acetates or selection of power points lies ready. In the midst of the second song your pastor gently whispers, "I feel the Holy Spirit is telling me to take over at this point." How do you feel? Do you resent his invasion of your ministry patch? Do you question his leading? Or do you quietly step aside, believing that the Holy Spirit sometimes does the unexpected? It happens. It happened to an Old Testament choir (2 Chronicles 5:13 and 14) and to a modern one – in New York's Brooklyn Tabernacle. Halfway through a service Pastor Jim Cymbala felt the Spirit telling him to preach. The church's famous choir was reaching the end of its first piece when he signalled that he wanted to take over before they sang again. At this unexpected point in the service he preached and gave an appeal, and then numbers of people responded.

Several days later a letter arrived from a family who had been in the meeting but had to leave early to catch a flight. "If you hadn't changed the order of service," they said, "we would have missed the message, but because you preached when you did our wayward son heard the Gospel and came to Christ." It happens because the Holy Spirit knows best.

You're an elder in a growing church. You bring years of Christian experience and expertise as a business executive to your leadership meetings. Your pastor has a powerful ministry in evangelism that is making a city-wide impact. The National Leadership Team has visited the church and highly commended it, and you can see a mega-ministry future for him. Then one day he announces he feels led to leave the city for ministry in an obscure rural area. You shake your head in disbelief and try to dissuade him. From your perspective he is making a seriously flawed career choice. Yet later you hear that, from that remote area, he has had an international influence. He has

85

touched the life of a prominent member of a foreign government and is still moving under the direction of the Holy Spirit. You can read the original details of that scenario in Acts 8:12f. It happens because the Holy Spirit knows best.

You're a pastor. You are conscientious and have carefully planned the afternoon's schedule of visiting. Suddenly, you have an urge to visit a backslidden man. You argue: "But Lord, he's said he doesn't want to be visited... he'll be angry if I do... and in any case I've got these other calls to make... besides, it's the other side of the town... and time is precious!" But the inner call persists, and reluctantly you obey. You go to the man's house. His sister opens the door. "Thank God you've come," she cries, "Jim is dying and he's calling out for someone to help him get right with God!" Humbly, you kneel at his bed and lead him back to Christ. You nearly missed it – but for the Holy Spirit. It happens because the Holy Spirit knows best.

The book of Acts is the story of Holy Spirit "interference" in which he causes unexpected people to do unexpected things in unexpected places with unexpected results (read Acts 2:1-13; 8:26f; 9:11f; 10:9f; 13:1-4; 16:6-10, for examples).

Calling his work "interference" simply means that, so often, God's ways are not our ways, and so we frequently misread what he is doing and are slow to respond to his prompting. But as Jesus pointed out to Nicodemus (John 3:7 and 8), what the Spirit does in human lives is as sovereignly free, as inscrutable and unpredictable as the wind, and unless we set our sails to the prevailing winds of his lordship in our lives and our churches, we will never experience his liberating, life-giving energy.

Because, after all, the Holy Spirit really does know best!

## Moving in the Flow of the Spirit

What is the secret of church growth? The answers are many and varied, yet many churches, in spite of sincere attempts at applying the recommended principles, see little evidence of growth. Why?

Maybe the answer does not lie so much in our failed methods, or our lack of resources in finances and manpower. Perhaps it lies at a deeper level: our real relationship with the Holy Spirit.

One of the most significant statements about the growth of the early church is found in Acts 9:31: *"Walking in the fear of the Lord and the comfort of the Holy Spirit, it multiplied"* (ESV).

The verse focuses on two factors. Firstly, on the church's part, there was an awesome sense of the holiness of God that moved them to walk the moral and spiritual tightrope with extreme watchfulness. And, secondly, on God's part, there was the "comfort" of the Holy Spirit that infused life and power into them and also controlled every aspect of their operation. These two factors released the flow of supernatural power that brought about inevitable growth.

Perhaps we have concentrated too much on principles and not enough upon the Person whom God sent to take charge of the church. It is out of our personal and collective relationship with the Spirit that true spiritual and numerical growth takes place.

It is all too easy for us to ignore the Spirit. We ignore him when we fail to understand our complete dependence on him and don't even bother to seek his empowering presence. We ignore him when we don't pay attention to the Book he has written (a Bible Society survey has revealed that in an average church of 50 people, only ten read the Bible every day and only 30 per cent read it at all between Sundays!). Seven times Jesus urges us to listen to what the Spirit says (Revelation 2 and 3). If we are not reading his Word and not responding to his voice through the gifts of the Spirit, and if we are ignoring the prompting of his voice within us, is it any wonder our prayer meetings don't achieve much? See Zechariah 7:11-13.

It is possible for us to resist the Spirit (Acts 7:51). Frequently he challenges our traditions and our preconceived ideas, our preferences and our prejudices. The early church prospered because it was willing to obey the uncomfortable "comfort" of the Spirit, abandoning old ways, breaking into new territory and yielding to the lordship of the Spirit in every area of its life and ministry. To "fear the Lord" means obeying him.

Tragically, it is possible for us to grieve the Holy Spirit (Ephesians 4:30). It is not so much our lack of resources that inhibits us, but our failure to live holy lives. The major cause of the lack of blessing lies here. The Spirit recoils from the acrid smoke of our pride, and the offensive odour of morally unwashed saints who sing, "Come just as you are to worship", but fail to deal with the critical spirit, jealousy, self-seeking, unforgiveness and secret sin that stains them. They forget that God requires clean hands, a pure heart, undivided loyalty of soul, and a mouth that is free from pious pretence (Psalm 24:3-6).

Finally, we can so easily quench the Spirit (1 Thessalonians 5:17). The Pentecostal Fire Brigade is always on standby. Nervous saints reach for fire extinguishers at the least spark of the supernatural, and control-freak leaders, often driven by pride and fear, react at the least sign of things getting out of (their) hands. But see Romans 12:11 and 2 Timothy 1:6.

We can ignore, resist, grieve or quench the Spirit. But if we desire true New Testament church growth, we must move in the flow of his purpose and power. After all, he's been "doing church growth" for the last 2,000 years. He does know how it's done!

## Riding the Thermals of the Spirit

In a stunning piece of TV footage, a brightly coloured paraglider hung seemingly motionless among the towering peaks of the Andes mountains. Just beyond him, a condor hovered, spreading its huge black wings against the blue of the sky. Then, suddenly, both bird and man soared skyward, borne by invisible currents of warm air. Riding the thermals, they became a fascinating illustration of the power of "powerless" flight.

Watching it, I remembered an occasion when, through the gifts of the Spirit, a local church was given an imaginative insight into the possibilities open to it through responding to "the thermals of the Spirit". The concept of the Christian life in terms of flight, rising as a bird does on the unseen movements of thermal currents, gives a feeling of vitality and mobility, of true aspiration and freedom, of exhilaration in the exploration of the wide open spaces of the spiritual realm. "Soar we now where Christ hath led, / Following our exalted Head."

To this we have been called: *"It is for freedom that Christ has set us free"* (Galatians 5:1). We are no longer caged in earth-bound captivity, we are called to the heights. The sky's the limit!

Too many Christians, however, live like spiritual moles, grubbing away through dark tunnels of earthly ambition – their time/space restricted goals of professional, social and material achievement – instead of enjoying the freedom of the lark that "arising from sullen earth, sings hymns at heaven's gate". Such an attitude is as absurd as that of an eagle swooping to join a rat race. We need to realise to what species we belong; to see our true identity as men and women adapted by grace to live *"in the heavenly places"* (Ephesians 1:3; 2:6).

The "thermals of the Spirit" are those occasions when he moves within us, perhaps through a verse of Scripture, a sentence in a sermon, the words of a hymn or song, a word through the gifts of the Spirit, or an indefinable inner prompting which moves us to praise or pray, write a letter, lift the phone or decide to act in a particular way. They sometimes come through some deep personal experience, joyous or tragic, which has a profound effect upon us. The movements of the Spirit, who, like the wind, *"blows where he wills"* (John 3:8), provide a particular upward thrust to lift us nearer to God and into a higher dimension of spiritual experience. It is vital that we take advantage of them.

The impulse to pray should never be postponed to "some more convenient time"; the response to some challenge of the Word of God should never be deferred. As the winds of God lift our hearts to some new awareness of his grace, or blow us off our intended course in some unexpected direction, let us not be guilty of resisting him. These are spiritual thermals, unseen movements of the Spirit, which have the power to lift us into a higher level of encounter with the glory of God and a more meaningful relationship with him.

We need to learn the "aerodynamics" of the Spirit, to become more sensitive to the ever-changing patterns of his ceaseless activity, to respond to the upward law of gravity which will pull us Godward. In this context it is worth remembering that *"those who wait upon the Lord...shall mount up with wings like eagles"* (Isaiah 40:31, NKJV). Let us stretch our wings and feel for the thermals of the Spirit, listening to C Day Lewis's advice to the skylark: "Be strong your fervent soaring, your skyward air... Float up there where voice and wing are one. A singing star, a note of light!'

One thing is certain: that's where God wants us to be (Isaiah 57:15)!

## Grieving the Spirit

In 1877, a Methodist minister, Dr William Cooke, published the second edition of his book entitled *The Shekinah*, a fascinating study of the manifest presence of God in the Scriptures. On page 208 it contained the following strikingly prophetic paragraph:

"We may erect spacious chapels, we may increase in worldly influence, we may earnestly defend the truth, we may lay down our plans with sagacity, we may call for an educated and talented ministry, but without the Holy Spirit we shall decline amidst all our advantages." The deserted chapels standing bleakly on our city streets, sometimes turned into furniture warehouses or Hindu temples, are a stark reminder of the truth of those words.

Often, of course, there were external reasons for that decline – the shift of populations from town centres and the vast changes in the structure of society – but there were also other, more disturbing, internal reasons.

In some cases the rot began in the minister's study, where he no longer *"devoted himself to prayer and the Word of God"* (Acts 6:2-4), but was lured away by the latest trends in theology and ecclesiology; sometimes it happened because men were appointed as elders and deacons not because they were *"full of the Holy Spirit and wisdom"* (Acts 6:3, 5), but because of their social and professional status; sometimes the decline set in because the members of these growing churches, Laodicean-like (Revelation 3:14-15), became self-satisfied and spiritually careless. The truth is that when we continually *"grieve the Spirit"* (Ephesians 4:30) our decline and fall is inevitable.

We grieve the Spirit when we resist him (Acts 6:51), when preachers cut the cloth of the Word to meet modern fashions (2 Timothy 4:1-5), and when we quench his fire (1 Thessalonians 5:19-21). But, perhaps more than anything, he is grieved when the redeemed rebel against their Redeemer (Isaiah 63:9, 10).

91

That "rebellion" is rarely expressed with a shaking fist, or in blatant worldliness, but in a quiet refusal to respond to God's call for holiness. Paul's warning about grieving the Spirit is set in a passage that deals with the subtle sins that undermine personal integrity, damage relationships and *"give opportunity to the devil"* (Ephesians 4:25-32).

Sadly, these things which short-circuit the flow of the Spirit's power can be found in many churches – in leaders as much as in the members.

When we glibly sing "Come just as you are to worship", we need to remember that God looks to see if our upraised hands are clean (Psalm 24:4-6; Hebrews 12:28, 29). Repentant sinners may truly sing "Just as I am", but recalcitrant saints must understand that, if they *"approve what God condemns"*, the Lord will not listen to them (Psalm 66:18).

Many churches blame their lack of success on their lack of resources in terms of buildings, personnel, money, etc., but frequently the real reason lies in the fact that the Holy Spirit of God recoils from what goes in the private lives, personal relationships and public behaviour of some of the leaders and members of those churches and withdraws from them. We must not underestimate the effects of personal sin.

In our humanness, sinless perfection may well be beyond us, but we must maintain the critical tension between sin-sensitivity and grace-awareness (1 John 1:8–2:1). Yes, we are justified by faith, but that does not mean we are free to ignore God's call for holiness. Constantly we must search our hearts and keep open to the probing of the Word and the Spirit (2 Corinthians 13:5). Otherwise, the dry rot of sinful compromise will grow, unseen but deadly, in the fabric of our churches and our own lives. Those empty chapels warn us against spiritual complacency, lest in the midst of today's apparent success we sow the seeds of tomorrow's decline.

## *The Decline and Fall of an 'Apostle'*

In his Talking Cricket column in the *Daily Telegraph*, Simon Hughes once referred to "a moment of immense symbolism on the South Australian coast," when one of the "Twelve Apostles", a group of giant limestone stacks that have protruded from the sea for thousands of years, collapsed beneath the waves. Hughes pointed out that, "the damage had been done imperceptibly over many centuries as the relentless Southern Ocean and the blasting winds gradually eroded the formation, but the end was swift."

For Simon Hughes, the symbolism had cricketing connotations, but there are significant implications for individual Christians and for the Church. The fall of an "apostle" immediately recalls the incredible story of Judas, a man who for three years lived in intimate companionship with the Son of God – only to betray him and then commit suicide.

Two significant verses in John 13 encapsulate in a matter of hours a process that had been going on for years. What began as a suggestion (verse 2) grew into a terrible reality (verse 27). The fall of Judas was not due to a sudden, overwhelming crisis, but was the outcome of a slow process of erosion in which his love for and commitment to Jesus gradually were challenged and finally mastered by other things.

"Where assault has failed, attrition may tell," wrote C. Day Lewis in a poem describing the power of the elements in *Absolute Cliffs*. And the story of Samson warns us that a man may be endued with supernatural power and exercise a "signs and wonders ministry" but still, through the neglect of the day-by-day disciplines of biblical living, succumb to the subtle whispers of Delilah. Such a man may continue to go through the well-practised routines of his "ministry" without realising that he has lost the essential "anointing"!

Through neglect of biblical principles, so-called apostolic ministry can end in collapse – and so can churches and denominational groups! Like the church in Galatia (Galatians 3:l-3), they may be born out of a genuine work of the Word and the Spirit and then, in time, revert to what Paul calls the "flesh". There is a subtle erosion of the original strongly-biblical, Christ-centred, and Spirit-controlled condition and its replacement by man-made alternatives.

For the Galatians, that meant embracing Judaism. For the second-generation Church it meant moving from the Spirit-led to the institutional. For the modern Church there is always the danger of moving away from a strong biblically-based foundation, which insists on applying scriptural tests to teaching and methods, to a pragmatic emphasis in which the question is, "Does it work?" rather than, "Is it biblically true?"

The "winds of change" are not always beneficial. In a slightly different context, Paul warns about doctrinal winds that create havoc (Ephesians 4:14). It is not always huge theological earthquakes that undermine the "white cliffs" of orthodox doctrine and biblical conduct, but almost imperceptible concessions to the spirit of the age.

The coastline that marked the frontiers between the Church and the world crumbles, and there are no clear-cut distinctions any more. The map of spiritual life is re-drawn by quiet adjustments to contemporary thinking and lifestyle fashions.

Significantly, in January 2002, one of America's leading Christian magazines, *Charisma*, stated: "Ten of the ministry leaders we featured on the covers of the magazine in the 1980s eventually endured embarrassing scandals. And two of the mega-churches we featured disbanded because of moral failures."

It added, "What seems to glitter with success today may not stand the heat of God's refining fire tomorrow." When the first apostles declared, *"We will give ourselves continually to prayer and the ministry of the word"* (Acts 6:4), they were laying the foundation of enduring "apostolic ministry". We need to take heed. There are no reliable alternatives.

## *Who Do You Think You Are?*

This title has been taken from the popular BBC1 programme in which well-known people search for their ancestors, giving fresh stimulus to the widespread growth of whole forests of family trees.

Tracing your roots is fascinating, though sometimes disconcerting. Turning the pages of old albums, with their sepia-toned photos of church events showing men with moustaches, wearing trilby hats and long coats, accompanied by women in pudding basin hats and smiling slightly self-conscious smiles, causes not a little amusement to their much more sophisticated 21$^{st}$ century descendants.

It's all rather quaint, like the old yellow Elim chorus books and red *Redemption* hymnbooks that make modern musicians smile faintly and whisper, "Did they really sing stuff like that in those days?" Incidentally, what will the people of 2057 say about us? Good grief!

Speaking to a large audience of Pentecostal leaders, Jack Hayford once said, "Never despise the past, for the past has brought you to where you are today." Sometimes we need to examine our roots in order to safeguard future fruits.

I was reminded of all this while reading the fascinating and perceptive account of Elim's early days in James Robinson's book, *Pentecostal Origins 1907–1925: Early Pentecostalism in Ireland in the Context of the British Isles* – a thought-provoking read.

Tracing your family tree sometimes produces some unexpected ancestors. It is certainly true that the Pentecostal movement grew out of some very tangled roots. A strange mixture of men and movements, teachings and practice, contributed to its history; yet amid much confusion, both theologically and pragmatically, God was at work. Where human unwisdom abounded, divine grace did much more abound.

Looking back, we can thank God for the caution of the founding fathers of Elim and others who, amid a great deal of fanaticism, laid the foundations of the movements they led on biblical principles. It is noteworthy that in 1916 George Jeffreys, in a booklet entitled *What We Believe*, wrote: "We can expect the onslaught of the enemy to be furious in his seeking to counterfeit and to produce extravagances which we must be careful to avoid by continuing steadfastly in God's precious Word."

We may truly thank God for those Pentecostal pioneers who stood for the truth and sought to found their teaching and their practice on the Word of God, refusing to be blown about by every wind of doctrine which happened to be swirling around them. They didn't get everything right, and they were very much people of their time, but they understood that the Word and the Spirit are essential to any true New Testament experience of spiritual life and humbly sought to move within those parameters.

Their manner of dress and their forms of worship may sometimes seem somewhat antequated to sophisticated modern eyes, but their desire to respond to the Holy Spirit within biblical restraints, their emphasis on biblical standards of holiness, and their passionate ambition to evangelise make them ancestors to be proud of and examples to emulate.

The contrary winds of questionable doctrines and dubious practice are still blowing around us. So-called 'new insights', often influenced by modern philosophical ideas, produce new doctrinal emphases and fashionable trends in 'doing church', but while we must be open to all that God is doing in our day we must also exercise the same perceptiveness that characterised our spiritual ancestors.

Sepia-coloured they may appear to us, but they were focused on God and their roots were in the Word and the Spirit. We must do the same, otherwise a coming generation will shake their heads over the faded colours of our own confident claims to be better than our fathers.

# *Re-discovering Our Pentecostal Roots*

In the early days of the Charismatic movement, at a meeting in which people from various denominations had gathered, I was approached by a mother and her young son. Indicating the eight or nine year-old, the mother exclaimed, "He's had it!" I was not quite sure what "it" was and my uncertainty must have registered for she went on to explain: "You know, he's had the baptism — and he speaks in tongues!" The boy nodded, "Yep!" he said. Tempted to shake my head over the naivety of these "new Charismatics", I was somewhat chastened by the memory of a "waiting meeting" where a group of "classical Pentecostals" praying for someone seeking "the baptism" nodded significantly at one another as she began to utter some words in tongues and whispered, "She's through!" It was as though the girl had obtained her spiritual "A Levels"! Actually, she wasn't "through", she was only at a starting point.

While not doubting the validity of the experience these two young people had, one has to question the mindset that seemed to treat the baptism in the Spirit as something to "get" – like a collector's item which would enhance their spiritual standing. The fact that he's "had it" and she's "through" is good news – so long as we understand that the baptism in the Spirit is not a status symbol but a doorway into an on-going relationship with the third Person of the Trinity with far-reaching consequences for us individually and the church to which we belong.

In a timely and thought-provoking article in the *Direction* magazine, Elim's Director of Training, Nigel Tween, has called for a fresh emphasis on the importance of the baptism in the Spirit. We may not wish to see a return to some of the old ways of doing things, but there is a danger that are we not actually encouraging people to seek for an authentic New Testament experience of being baptised in the Spirit. There seems a vagueness about some current claims to being filled with the Spirit. People talk of being "blessed" or of "soaking" in the Spirit, and of other feel-good experiences, but at times there seems little evidence of an Acts 1:8 enduement with power as the dynamic leading to effective witness to Christ.

As Nigel Tween rightly says, leaders need to teach Pentecostal truth and encourage New Testament practice, otherwise we are in danger of losing our Pentecostal distinctiveness and squandering our Pentecostal inheritance. The word "Pentecostal" on our notice boards and our headed notepaper is merely a misnomer if it is not matched by what is happening in our pulpits and in the people who gather in our churches. In that case, we are guilty of transgressing the "Trades Description Act"! We need to believe our beliefs, proclaim our doctrines, practise what we preach, and understand that the baptism in the Spirit is not just a personal spiritual luxury to be enjoyed but an essential empowerment helping us minister to a world living in the wasteland of a moral and spiritual wilderness.

We need to seek fresh ways of helping people into a genuine "Acts 2" experience of the baptism in the Spirit; we need to seek more appropriate and meaningful ways of encouraging and exercising the gifts in the Spirit; we need to stress the fact that the baptism in the Spirit is not a terminus at which we reach our goal, but a departure platform from which we travel on the next phase of the spiritual journey leading towards our true destination in the purposes of God.

While we are thankful for the fresh insights that others have brought to the doctrine of the Spirit, we must not allow ourselves to be diverted from the sound biblical truths that gave birth to the Pentecostal movement and have sustained its validity and vitality through the years. There is a danger that, in being over-influenced by the latest trends in theology and practice, we will move away from the Christ-centred, biblically-based, Spirit-empowered "Foursquare Gospel" of our founding fathers with their passionate zeal to evangelise the lost. That is something we must not do.

# The Next Generation Must Look to its Spirit-filled Heritage to Realise its Destiny

The old story of Isaac re-opening the wells his father had dug and giving them their original names (Genesis 26:14-22) is not misty-eyed nostalgia. It's a statement of important truth: no new generation can afford to ignore the truths and spiritual principles of its historic past if it is to secure its future destiny.

I was reminded of that story while looking afresh at the roots of the modern Pentecostal movement and reading across a fairly wide range of writers for and against the teaching for which our founding fathers stood and often suffered. Somehow it seems important to restate those foundational truths.

It is impossible within the scope of this short article to go into any in-depth analysis, but one thing becomes very clear: the "experts", while airily dismissing the early Pentecostals as theologically inept, often disagree among themselves and, at times, interpret the Scriptures in very arbitrary ways. I found myself inserting question marks in the margins of most of these books!

To a thoughtful observer, all this might seem slightly amusing, like watching a pride of learned lions wrestling in the safety of their dens in some theological safari park. But the problem is that some of these writers, because of their reputation as "evangelical scholars", have caused some Pentecostals to abandon the "old wells" of well-proven spiritual truth and empowerment.

Among such writers there is a great deal of discussion as to the meaning of the word "baptism", the "timing" of the gift of the Spirit, whether it was coincident with or subsequent to the conversion of those who received it, the nature of tongues, and the theological perspectives of Luke and Paul and so on.

The truth of the matter is that, while the early Pentecostals, caught up in the incoming tide of the Spirit, may not have had the time for deeper reflection and precise evaluation in their teaching and may sometimes have got things wrong, they did recapture the dynamic experience of New Testament Christianity. And that is what we are in danger of losing. Ponder Paul's warning to a Pentecostal church in Galatians 3:3-5.

We may so concentrate on analysing the semantics, theology, chronology, geography, history and psychology of it all that we miss the essential reality. The fact is that the New Testament Church was vibrantly alive. Jesus himself said that the coming of the Spirit would be like *"rivers of living water"* flowing out of the innermost being, not some invisible, subterranean stream meandering imperceptibly in the depths of the personality (John 7:37, 38), and when the Spirit came he was *"poured out"*.

People were *"filled"*, he *"fell upon"* believers and there were clear manifestations of his coming – people *"received power"*, and *"spoke with tongues and prophesied"*. The presence of the Spirit was vividly manifested in the preaching, worship, fellowship, personal lifestyle and passionate evangelism of the early Church, so that visitors who came into their meetings confessed that *"God is really in your midst"* (1 Corinthians 14:25).

It was this sense of a dynamic collective and personal encounter with the Holy Spirit, experienced evidentially, that enabled the early Church – and their Pentecostal descendants – emphatically to say, *"This is that spoken of by the prophet Joel"*.

Nothing short of the same definitive New Testament experience of the baptism and infilling of the Holy Spirit will enable their 21st century grandchildren to enjoy their heritage and realise their destiny. We dare not opt for less – and the wells are still there waiting for us!

## *Show Your Power, O Lord!*

**W**e sing songs, clap and ask the Lord for a visitation – but how prepared are we?

Morning sunshine shone through stained glass windows, filling a beautifully decorated church with summer brightness. The congregation consisted of a wide range of age groups, and to judge from their attire many of them were on holiday. The worship leader (like policemen, how young they look these days) might have been on holiday too, to judge from his rather baggy tee shirt and the casualness of his manner.

We sang some fairly ancient worship songs (what a short "shelf life" a lot of modern songs have) but we also sang some pleasing newer ones with meaningful words and, thankfully, singable tunes. Then we launched into "Show Your power, O Lord." It's a great song, with its prayer for divine visitation which will reveal God's justice to the nations, move the church to action, and "set the people free." As we sang I looked around at this fairly average evangelical / charismatic church and wondered what would happen if, to use the modern jargon, God did "show up." There we were, in a nice comfortable building, a nice, comfortable group of people singing nice, comfortable thoughts to a nice, comfortable tune – but what if God answered? To be honest, I wondered whether it was all a bit too casual. Did I, for one, really want God to show his power just then – with the thought of roast beef and Yorkshire pudding only an hour away? Were my fellow worshippers really wanting it to happen, or was it a hazy dream-like notion trembling on a distant horizon? In all truth, they didn't appear particularly anxious for a divine thunderstorm to happen on that Sunday morning.

It reminded me of a passage in Eugene Peterson's book, *The Gift*, where he quotes Annie Dillard's provocative question about contemporary attitudes to worship: "Why do we people in churches seem like cheerful, brainless tourists on a package tour of the absolute? ... Does anyone have the foggiest idea what sort of power we so blithely invoke?" Dillard goes on to suggest that we should be wearing crash helmets and be issued with life preservers and signal flares when we go to church because we are in the presence of a God of infinite power.

What do we really mean when we talk about God "showing his power"? Sometimes we seem like people who watch TV programmes about dramatic storms, fascinated by vivid scenes of thunder and lightening and awed by the power of tornados, but rather relieved to know that that kind of thing is not likely to happen here.

It is one thing to read Tommy Tenney's account in *The God Chasers* of the visitation of God in Houston, Texas – but would we really want that sort of thing to happen here? I mean, do we really want "divine thunderclaps" that send the pastor sprawling ten feet behind the platform, and meetings that go on and on for hour upon hour? Some of us look meaningfully at our watches if a meeting goes five minutes over time, and after all, what about missing *Match of the Day*? Do we really want the crying and tears, the "emotionalism", the confession of sin, the calls for repentance?

Isn't it odd how we get misty-eyed over accounts of revival in the days of Wesley and Whitefield, and not a little nostalgic about the "early days" of the Pentecostal movement, and yet become uneasy about some of the ways in which the power of God is manifested in our own day? Granted that there are times when what we call a "move of the Spirit" seems accompanied by evidence of fleshly excess; but that mixture of Spirit and flesh has been evident in all revivals. While we need to distinguish between the genuine and the counterfeit, we also need to make sure that our judgment is based on Bible principles, not personal preferences.

One of the significant things about the Pentecostal outpouring at the beginning of the last century was the fact that it was not only rejected but vehemently opposed by some of the very people who had been most passionate in praying for a new visitation of the Holy Spirit. They longed for revival but disliked the form in which it actually came. We too need to make sure that our desire for what we call "a move of God" is not limited by the same prejudices.

To sing or pray, "Show Your Power, O Lord," may be to open ourselves to a manifestation of his presence and power which will be a seismic shock that might seriously affect the "comfort zone" of our manageable spirituality. Like its natural counterpart, such a spiritual earthquake will have a devastating effect on our man-made structures of religious probity. The inrush of true revival will upturn our timetables, challenge our cherished traditions, storm the ramparts of our prejudices, demolish our pride, expose our hidden sins, and break us down before the cross, It will even make the British weep. Such movements come with a spiritual health warning: "This will seriously damage your pride"!

It would be interesting to conduct a survey into what the words, "the power of God", actually mean to the average Christian. Hazarding a guess, one would think that to many people they express ideas of signs and wonders, successful evangelism and, maybe, a vague sense of "blessing". "The mighty power of God" is perhaps conceived of by many in terms of wonderful healings and miracles, great multitudes of people being converted and filled with the Holy Spirit. To experience the power of God, for most people, is to be given "power for service", to experience the baptism in the Spirit and exercise the gifts of the Spirit, all of which may be true but surely falls short of the full implications hidden in the words.

Even the term "Show Your Power..." gives an impression of people watching a demonstration, like the observers of the first atom bomb watching through binoculars at a safe distance as the great mushroom cloud of nuclear power rises on the distant horizon. The very words may isolate us from the action. It is fascinating to read about, and watch on video, events in South America and other places where God is manifesting his powerful presence, but deep inside we are not so sure we would want to get caught up in the maelstrom of spiritual, and even physical upheaval, and schedule – shattering disruption, that real revival brings. To misquote an old hymn, "While on others Thou art calling, do not cause me stress."

Having said all that, let us ask another question: is the "mighty power of God" always to be thought of in terms of dramatic events? Is the supernatural always spectacular? The answer, obviously is "no". It was neither the earthquake, wind nor the fire that moved Elijah to bow before God, but the "still small voice". Power is not always measured by decibels or seismographs. A clapped out Ford with a broken silencer may make an impressive noise compared with the steady hum of the generators in a power station, but the output of energy is out of all proportion. From one there is only noise, from the other there is a release of power which brings light and heat and a host of other benefits to the city.

We preachers are partly to blame for this misconception about the power of God. To our delight, we noticed that the word "*dunamis*" in Acts 1:8 has a modern cousin named "dynamite" owing its ancestry to the same Greek root. So, although Alfred Nobel didn't discover the possibilities of dynamite until 1856, we cheerfully began to interpret the "power from on high" as dynamite – the explosive power that goes off with an impressive bang and blows things to bits. Nobel, incidentally, was so dismayed by what the world did with his discovery that, as an act of contrition he established the Nobel Peace Prize to counteract the destructive effects of his invention.

Of course there is a sense in which the power of the Spirit does explode within the ramparts of human pride and *"demolish strongholds"* (2 Corinthians 10:4,5,) and as we have seen, there are times when the *"mighty rushing wind"* of Acts 2 still sweeps across the spiritual landscape with awesome force, but we need to realize that the power of the Spirit does not always operate in such dramatic ways. As Jesus pointed out, the kingdom of God does not always come with impressive observable outward show, Luke 17:20.

That word *"power"* in Acts 1:8 could be more correctly defined as "the ability to make things happen"; it is creative energy released into people's lives in order to bring God's purposes into being. In the context of that particular passage it had to do with effective evangelism in terms of witnessing to Christ, but in its wider context it has to do with achieving God's saving and life-changing purpose in the lives of men and women. Equally dynamic, though less dramatic, the miracle of transformed lives remains as much an evidence of God at work as any visible or physical miracle.

God "shows his power" when he takes up a collection of adulterers, homosexuals, playboy no-goods, drunken louts, fraudulent business men, prostitutes, evil minded gossips, thieves and moral bankrupts, and changes them by his "ability to make things happen" into a group of people who, for all their faults, have *"been washed, sanctified, justified in the name of the Lord Jesus Christ and by the Spirit of our God,"* (1 Corinthians 6:9-11). It is probably true to say that the angels who *"desire to look into these things"* (1 Peter 1:12), are more impressed and excited by seeing the astonishing transformation of Saul the arch persecutor into Paul the great apostle than they are by physical signs and wonders. Maybe, we should be, too.

If God answers our prayers and "shows his power" we may well witness dramatic thunderstorms of supernatural manifestation, but we must also be prepared for moral earthquakes. What if the holiness of God challenges our less than honest ways of handling money which really belongs to him, as he did with Ananias and Sapphira (Acts 5:1-11)? What if he comes to us as he did to the seven churches in Asia Minor (Revelation 2 and 3 ) with an exposure of lovelessness, lifelessness and lukewarmness in our churches and in ourselves? What if he rips off our spiritual masks and shows us the unacceptable face of compromising Christianity? What if he "throws light into the darkened cells where passion reigns within... the chambers where polluted things hold empire o'er the soul'"? What if the consuming fire of his passionate holiness flames out against the pride and selfishness that forms so much of what we really are? What if he takes us at our word and the reverberations of his powerful presence cause the foundations of our complacency to shake?

"Show Your Power, O Lord!" Yes, Lord. Make your justice known amongst the nations. Deal with the tyrants, Lord, defend the powerless, establish the rule of righteousness. Move your church, Lord, send a mighty Holy Ghost revival, restore New Testament order and power to your people and set them free. Give us the liberty of the Spirit, Lord, send us apostolic leadership, make us a powerful presence in the world, send revival, Lord.

But go gently, Lord. Don't create too much disturbance. You know, we are rather busy, and we've got a full programme lined up – our five–year plan has only just been passed by the elders. Also, Lord, you know our culture. We don't like anything over the top – after all, we're not Americans! No excess, please, we're British! Show Your Power, Lord, but go easy!

Hmmm, I wonder!

# Liberty, Licence or Lordship?

*"The Gospel is too often presented as a spiritual paracetamol rather than a Divine call to repentance."*

Caught up in the horrors of the French Revolution, when a blood-red river of anger, hatred and revenge swept through the streets of Paris in the name of "Liberty, Equality and Fraternity," Madame Marie Jeanne Roland was driven to her death at the dreaded guillotine. As the tumbril rattled over the cobbled streets, she was heard to cry, "O Liberty! O Liberty! What crimes are committed in thy name!"

There are times when, surveying the crass abuse of "liberty" in the church, one is tempted to echo that cry. One of the most abused texts in the New Testament is 2 Corinthians 3:17, *"Now the Lord is the Spirit, and where the Spirit of the Lord is, there is freedom"* (NIV). It has been employed to justify behaviour which has ranged from the bewildered to the bizarre and has occasioned anarchy in the Kingdom of God.

Too often, such demands for liberty have meant "the freedom to please myself." In the exercise of the gifts of the Spirit, such an attitude often hides behind a mask inscribed, *"Quench not the Spirit when I am operating!"* The abuse of freedom in this way has brought the precious gifts of the Spirit into disrepute, often causing churches to discourage their use rather than suffer the selfishness and foolishness of people who were *"using their freedom as an occasion for the flesh"* rather than *"serving one another in love"* (Galatians 5:13).

That verse also has a powerful message for other people who adopt a fine "anti-legalism" pose. "I'm mature, and therefore no one is going to tell me what I can or cannot do." Even when faced by plain statements of the Scriptures, such people make their unilateral Declaration of Independence to the strains of, "We shall not be

107

moved." Like the extremists of the French Revolution, they destroy the true freedom, equality and brotherhood of God's people in their insistence on being free to "do their own thing." Such arrogance is foreign to the spirit of the New Testament.

It is not only at the personal level that the abuse of spiritual freedom takes place. It often occurs at leadership level, where Biblical constraints and restraints are ignored in an impatient pursuit of "success." The decline and fall of some powerful religious empires has taken place as a consequence of their desire to be free from what they saw as the inhibiting influence of biblical principles. In the name of "intellectual freedom" the modern church has frequently stepped beyond the parameters of biblical truth, in the name of "personal freedom" the standards of biblical holiness have been eroded, in the pursuit of "freedom of expression" and "relevance" New Testament guidelines for Christian life and practice to a large extent have been set aside.

The Holy Spirit has been side-lined. Even though we acknowledge his Deity and want his power, we want him on our own terms. We want his gifts and his blessing, we value his power, but only as the background to our own endeavours. The power of the Spirit is the "outboard motor" which gives extra thrust to our self-drive speedboats. We acknowledge his presence in our meetings with "a word of prayer" but give him little real opportunity to exercise his lordship, and our highly prized liberty becomes a straitjacket of spiritual ineffectiveness.

Only where the Spirit is Lord is there true freedom. That involves active obedience to his lordship. Our freedom on the roads is only possible when we obey the *Highway Code*. However restricting traffic lights and speed limits may be, we know, sometimes to our cost, that chaos, not freedom, results when we ignore their instructions. So it is spiritually.

The story of the early church is a vivid picture of what happens when the Holy Spirit is Lord – not simply theologically, but actually. It is one thing to sing, "He is Lord…" but quite another to accept the implications of that fact in personal terms.

### The Spirit Must be Lord of our Theology

If that sounds like stating the obvious, it is still needs to be said – and loudly – to the modern church. Why doesn't the Spirit *"confirm the Word with signs following"* today? Often because "the Word" preached, even in evangelical pulpits, is not "the Word" of the New Testament! He will not confirm what he has not inspired.

Too much modern preaching is influenced by modern trends, by media styles of communication and by what is perceived as human need. The Gospel is too often presented as a spiritual paracetamol rather than a divine call to repentance. The "modern trends" of the first century world were against the Gospel message – the Cross was offensive to Jewish theology and ridiculous to Greek philosophy – but Paul refused to become "relevant" by accommodating his theology to those trends (1 Corinthians 1:12-25). We must do the same.

In our Bible colleges and training programmes, in the studies of pastors and preachers there must be a renewed emphasis on the sole authority and sufficiency of Scripture. We must come with fresh urgency and earnestness to *"devote ourselves to prayer and the Word of God"* (Acts 6:2-4). Like Paul, we must rely on the Holy Spirit's instruction and enabling (1 Corinthians 2:1-5,12,13).

What a "crooked and depraved generation" needs is not the fireworks of slick media presentations and clever soundbites that appeal to its self-centreness, but the God-illumined starlight of men and women who are *"holding out the Word of life"* (Philippians 2:14-16).

Let us repeat it, "The Holy Spirit will only confirm with signs following the Word that he has inspired." And we can only preach that Word when through fervent prayer and earnest study of the Scriptures we open ourselves to what he wants to say. While it is right that we are conversant with and able to respond to modern insights, and while it is foolish to think that thoughtless Bible-punching is God-honouring, the fact remains that our society desperately needs to hear the Word of God preached in the power of the Spirit by men and women who have come fresh from the throne of God.

### The Spirit Must be Lord of Our Cultural Attitudes

To a deep-dyed nationalist like Peter, stepping across the threshold of a Gentile house was not only unthinkable but unlawful (Acts 10:9-14,28). It was as distasteful as eating non-kosher food. But the Holy Spirit demanded that Peter overcome his natural preferences and even his theological pre-conceptions and take a radically different attitude to people who, up until now he had considered "dogs." His "anti-gentilism" was as unacceptable to God as the anti-semitism of Haman in Esther's day.

Not until Peter got rid of these cultural and racial biases could he be used in the Spirit's on-going purposes (Acts 10:28f). In days when, in spite of the ambitions of European politicians, nationalism is still a powerful and destructive force, we need to catch the Spirit's "world-view" and be willing to break across the racial, cultural and social prejudices which embitter and estrange our world. We must not allow our natural fear and dislike of militant Islam to prejudice us against our Muslim neighbours, nor our abhorrence of the often aggressive homosexual lobby to harden our hearts against our fellow human beings, many of whom struggle with their sexuality, and who need, just as much as anybody, the redeeming grace of God. Under the Holy Spirit's leading we must be willing to cross the threshold with the good news about Jesus.

## *The Spirit Must be Lord of Our Church Agendas*

The secret of the early church lay in the active, often intrusive, lordship of the Holy Spirit. He confirmed the Word with signs following, not only because they preached what they received from him, but because they went where he told them to go and did what he told them to do. This was the original "First Direct" spiritual banking enterprise. All the resources of God were at their disposal so long as they kept in touch and followed his instructions.

The lordship of the Spirit in the book of Acts is remarkable. He it was who insisted that Philip leave a highly successful "city-wide crusade" for a spot of one to one evangelism in the Gaza desert (Acts 8) – what on earth did the "crusade committee" make of that? He it was who made Peter "break the rules" and enter a Roman house (Acts 10). He it was who insisted, probably much to the discomfort of the "church session" at Antioch, on selecting their best men for a new initiative in evangelism (Acts 13:1-4). He it was who refused permission for Paul and his team to preach in Asia and positively forbade them to go to Bithynia, because he wanted to "church plant" in Europe (Acts 16:6-10).

Without doubt, the Spirit was the real "Director of Evangelism" in the days of the Acts – and he was so because they recognized his lordship and submitted to it, not only theoretically but practically. For them, "Apostolic ministry" was not realized in globe-trotting mega-ministries, but in devoting themselves to prayer and the ministry of the Word (Acts 6:4). Consequently, their decision-making, choices of people, evangelistic strategies and church-building methods were not the product of their own cleverness, or even of their unique experience in the work of God, but the result of the Holy Spirit's direct involvement in their affairs. It was his agenda, not theirs, that determined their course. The book of Acts reveals this outstanding emphasis on prayer; Acts 1:14,24, 2:1; 4:23f; 6:4; 10:9; 13:1-4,

14:23; 16:16-25; 20:36. He blessed their work because they did it his way.

Too often we have reversed the biblical order. We have come to God asking him to rubber stamp our ideas instead of genuinely seeking to know his agenda; not with Brother Bloggs "opening with a word of prayer, please," but with sustained, prayerful and thoughtful openness to what the Spirit is saying to his church. Too often the brilliant "brain children" on which we dote are either prematurely born or illegitimate. We need to get it right, to realize that, in this as in everything, *"that which is born of the flesh is flesh,"* and only that which is *"born of the Spirit is spirit."* That only happens when we understand that the lordship of the Spirit is more than a nice idea.

The secret of the early church's success is nowhere more plainly explained than in Acts 9:31 *"Walking in the fear of the Lord, and the comfort of the Holy Spirit, they were multiplied."* Out of a deep reverence for God created by their awareness of his holiness, and their own utter dependence upon him, they walked humbly and obediently in accordance with his will, and they experienced the "comfort" of the Holy Spirit. That "comfort" was more than mere consolation. The word means "to encourage, help, enable, strengthen, fortify." From him they received not only direction but dynamic (Acts1:8).

At times he was an uncomfortable Comforter, disturbing their comfort zones, breaking into their conferences with his own ideas, interfering with their preconceived plans, selecting his own personnel and insisting on having his own way in everything. But when he was truly Lord the real revolution began, and in it they found true liberty, equality and fraternity – and it was wonderful. It always is!

# True Fellowship

Some years ago, a group of aerodynamics engineers, intrigued by the fact that wild geese always seemed to fly in a "V" formation, made a fascinating discovery. I quote: "As the geese fly in the 'V' formation, the flapping of the wings of each bird gives an uplift to the ones before and behind him, and he in turn received an uplift from them. This 'lift' creates approximately 70% more forward thrust, so that as a group the geese can fly further than they could do so individually. If one goose slips out of formation and tries to fly on his own, he gives and receives nothing."

Once again, nature provides us with a brilliant parable. We need each other! Trying to go it alone is not only unscriptural, it just doesn't work. It is significant that Isaiah's words about spiritual high-flyers (40:31) contains vital plurals – *"those who hope in the Lord will renew their strength. They will soar upon wings as eagles. They will run and not grow weary, they will walk and not faint."*

"Fellowship" is one of the most often used terms in describing early church life: *"All the believers were together"* (Acts 2:44). As John Wesley remarked, "The New Testament knows nothing of solitary religion." And even an intrepid high-flyer like the apostle Paul knew that he could not go it alone. With all his spiritual and intellectual powers – and the fact that he had boldly gone up into the spiritual stratosphere where no one else had been (2 Corinthians 12: 1f) – he recognised his dependence on the aerodynamic thrust provided by his friends and colleagues (Romans 16, for instance), and repeatedly called upon ordinary church members to pray for him (Ephesians 6:18,19; Colossians 4:3; 1 Thessalonians 5:25; 2 Thessalonians 3:10).

Such "togetherness", however, does not merely mean belonging to the same church or meeting in the same building, or turning up at the same meetings. Too often fellowship seems to mean little more than a friendly nod towards a few recognised faces before we slip out of church into the comfortable anonymity of our own privacy.

But that is not what the New Testament word means. It means building relationships – actually getting to know one another, loving one another, talking to one another, caring for one another, bearing one another's burdens, and working together with one another in the local church in a shared vision for the kingdom of God in a challenging world. It means opening the frontiers of our private world to people who would otherwise be strangers. It means keeping in formation, like the wild geese, giving and receiving strength through fellowship, moving in the same direction and helping one another forward in the flight path of the Spirit.

Are you providing "uplift" or "down-drag"? Are people encouraged to love Jesus more through meeting you? Or are they discouraged by your negative attitudes? Do you contribute to the forward thrust of your church through your enthusiastic involvement – your prayers, your giving, your practical support, your personal encouragement? Or are you merely "flapping about" in lonely individualism?

Some of us need to get back into formation!

## What Hamlet and Narcissus Say to the Church

**W**riting about a new production of Shakespeare's play *Hamlet*, Sir Richard Eyre, the former Director of the National Theatre, said "The play was a mirror of our age, obsessed with celebrity and marinated in narcissism". He quoted Hamlet's last words, "The rest is silence", and commented, "For him there is nothing after death; it's a void, an absence of meaning. It's hard to find a more contemporary sentiment." Our age is indeed obsessed with celebrity. Celebrity chefs and cooks fill our screens and bookshops with amazing recipes; celebrity sportsmen dazzle with their skills; stars of screen and stage, pop stars and politicians, musicians, media people and writers (many of whom have a lot to say, but whose lavish lifestyles are a flamboyant attempt to cover the nakedness of their own moral poverty) become the role models of a generation seeking to find the meaning of its existence.

It is this yearning for reality that so often produces what Eyre calls "narcissism". Narcissus was the young man in the Greek fable who became so infatuated with himself that, spurning all other loves, he faded away and became the flower that bears his name. Absorbed in himself, he lost himself. This is a warning for our contemporary "me" generation, preoccupied with its looks, its status, its possessions, its ambitions, its health and its desires for personal happiness, and at the same time, haunted by the fear of failure, ill-health and advancing age, creeps nervously through the valley of the shadow of death. No wonder, then, that what someone has called "the psychotherapy industry" is the fastest growing sector of medicine today, or that prescriptions for anti-depressant medications are at an all-time high, and the abuse of illicit drugs and alcohol is rampant. It is an age, for all its self-conscious pretensions, *"without hope and without God in the world"* (Ephesians 2:12). Yet, too often, the Church seems unable to minister effectively to the world because it is weakened by a strain of the very same virus from which the world suffers. It, too, has an "obsession with celebrity". It elevates men who are deemed to be charismatic leaders, outstanding personalities, or are seen to possess special ministry gifts, and gives them, their words and actions, an authority and prominence that tends to shift the focus away from the Lord Jesus Christ and subtly undermines his lordship as head of the Church. The cult of personality, as Paul pointed out in 1 Corinthians 3:3-7, is a tell-tale symptom of the virus of worldliness.

If the charge of "narcissism" seems to be an unfair diagnosis of modern Christianity, just have a look at the emphasis on problem-solving, personal happiness and self-fulfilment themes in much of the books, preaching, and teaching materials, conferences and seminars, which top the popularity charts in today's Christian world. The emphasis on "counselling" in a great deal of modern ministry echoes the rise of psychotherapy in the world. Modern Christians seem to want therapy rather than theology – to have their own perceived needs met rather than to meet God in his Word, and then, in the life-giving power of his Spirit, go out to live and minister for him in that broken world outside the Church. Many seem to be holy hypochondriacs, absorbed in themselves and their personal needs and happiness, always taking their spiritual temperature, worried over their pulse rate, and forever seeking the latest ministry wonder-drug that will alleviate their symptoms, instead of quietly walking with God on a day-to-day basis of trust and obedience (Micah 6:8; Philippians 4:4-9).

Of course we should honour men whom God is using and blessing with his favour; of course there are those among us who really do need patient counselling; but when we shift our focus from Jesus Christ to men, and when we become so absorbed with ourselves, our man-centredness and self-centredness rob Jesus of his glory, the church of its full potential, and a desperate world of genuine Spirit-directed and empowered ministry. "The rest," as Hamlet said, "is silence." Apart from Jesus Christ, his cross and risen power manifested through his church, there is nothing else to be said.

## *Welcome to the Submerging Church*

It was intended as a light-hearted remark during a conversation between friends but suddenly it assumed rather more serious overtones, or perhaps "undertones" would be more accurate, as the implications became clearer. "Did you know," said one of the group, pointing to the others, "that he belongs to the 'Submerging Church'"?

Together they laughed at the intended play on words, but then they began to toy with the implications lying behind the active present tense of such a title: not "submerged" (sunk, wrecked), but "submerging" (moving beneath the surface, exploring deeper waters). Perhaps there was more to it than met the eye.

With a penchant for impressive titles, over the years churches and movements have called themselves all sorts of things in attempting to state their special vision or underline their superior version of the faith. 1 Corinthians 1:10-14 reminds us that one-upmanship based on personalities and special doctrinal emphases or ways of "doing church" have plagued the Church from its beginning. There is a certain pride in belonging to a certain stream of spirituality – especially if it is called "this great new thing that God is doing" – as if he had never thought of it before!

Submarines do not have too much superstructure – this enables them to boldly go where cruise liners and supertankers never can. Likewise, the submerging church is more concerned with exploring "the deep things of God" than building bigger battleships. It knows that, in the end, exploration will reveal and release knowledge which will profoundly affect what happens up on the surface of things.

The submerging church does not belong to any one particular "navy"; it sails under different flags and from various ports, but its crews have one thing in common – they have a passionate desire to glorify God through knowing him in depth and opening themselves up to his Word and his Spirit at levels which will profoundly affect how they worship, conduct their fellowship, live their personal lives and witness to the world. They are not part of any particular network; they are simply churches of various descriptions whose leaders and people, humbly dissatisfied with their present spiritual condition, are searching the Scriptures and prayerfully seeking to be open to what the Spirit is saying to them. They do not ignore what is happening in other places, but they are neither defenders of tradition nor devotees of trends – they just want to know what God is saying to them in their particular part of his kingdom.

Submerging churches are captained by leaders whose apostolic priority is to give themselves to prayer and the Word of God (Acts 6:2-4), because they know that this, above all, will enable them to fulfil their calling in leading their church in the direction God desires. In Eugene Petersen's words, they are "contemplative pastors" who know their first responsibility is "to dive into the ocean of prayer". Their crews are people who come to church not simply to do what they normally do on Sunday mornings but to say, *"We are all here in the presence of God to hear whatever the Lord has told you to tell us"* (Acts 10:33). Beyond the superficialities of modern life, they are people who desire, with the Spirit's aid, *"to search the deep things of God"* (1 Corinthians 2:6-16), and open their inmost beings to his promises and purposes for them individually and collectively.

Out of those in-depth encounters with God the submerging church begins to worship *"in Spirit and in truth"*. Its worship is stirred not by musical rhythms but by divine revelation; and out of that deep exposure to the heart of God, where *"deep calls unto deep"*, it experiences life-changing encounters and finds itself propelled into the dark depths where the "fish" are. The love of Christ impels it *"to launch out into the deep"* and reach out imaginatively and dynamically *"to seek and to save those who are lost"*.

Yes, I know, submarines are not fishing boats, but in the realm of the Spirit all analogies break down somewhere because God's ways are bigger than ours. At least, it's worth thinking about!

## Beware the "Balaam Syndrome"

In an intriguing poem called *In Church*, Thomas Hardy draws a picture of a preacher in full flow, which, uncomfortably, is rather closer to reality than we might want to think. It's the picture of a powerful sermon in which the preacher's voice "thrills to the utmost tiles" and "emotion pervades the crowded aisles".

In the stunned silence that follows, he "glides to the vestry door and shuts it," or so he thinks. But, unknown to him, one of his Sunday School children who "adores him as one without gloss or guile," peeps at him as he stands before the mirror and "re-enacts... each pulpit gesture in deft dumb show." In other words, what the congregation thought was "powerful preaching of the Word," was actually a cleverly orchestrated piece of performance ministry – high on "artistic merit" but abysmally low on spiritual reality.

Thomas Hardy was a gloomy unbeliever who found it easy to ridicule the religion of his day, but his words in this poem have an uncomfortable resonance – they remind us that it is easy to put on a show of spirituality which doesn't actually ring true.

I was reminded of this poem when reading the story of Balaam. When you listen to his "philosophy of ministry" (recorded in Numbers 22:18,38; 23:8,12,26; 24:3,4,13), you feel that you are in the presence of a man who is totally committed to preaching the Word and who adamantly refuses any financial inducements to compromise his message. Here is a man of absolute integrity whose eloquent prophetic ministry carries a mighty anointing. On those terms he would be invited to speak at conferences all over the world.

Balaam seems above reproach but, on closer inspection, the Bible reveals that his donkey had more spiritual awareness than he did (Numbers 22:23-34). Moreover, in relation to his financial integrity, the divine Auditor finds serious discrepancies in his personal account (2 Peter 2:15,16; Jude 11). And though he makes a great play on the high moral ground he occupies, the monitors of the Spirit reveal a very different picture (Numbers 31:16; Revelation 2:14).

Unerringly, the Holy Spirit exposes the secret agenda lying beneath the public image. This man is not really what he would like us to believe.

## *Success Isn't Everything*

Scene one: Berlin, 1940. The German capital is jubilant following the conquest of most of Europe. Suddenly, an unknown Jewish preacher with an astonishing "near-death experience" visits the city warning that the judgment of God is about to fall on Nazi Germany. In the Reichstag, Adolf Hitler calls for a day of national repentance and prayer. Propaganda chief Goebbels broadcasts to the nation; Field Marshal Goering and Gestapo chief Himmler, together with other leaders, attend prayer meetings.

Impossible? In modern terms that is precisely what happened when the prophet Jonah preached in Nineveh, the capital of the notoriously evil Assyrian empire. See Jonah 3.

Scene two: Moscow, 1980s. A hotel room. Billy Graham sits head in hands after a highly successful city-wide crusade. The evangelist is unhappy. "Why did you send me here, God? These people have been enemies of the USA, their missiles are trained on the West; they have a history of horrific crimes against humanity; many of them are godless Communists, corrupt politicians, brutal KGB men, prison guards and the like. Why do you want to save them? They don't deserve mercy. I'm not at all happy with this." Impossible? Surely, for Billy Graham? "Scene two" didn't, of course, take place, but it's an imaginary picture of what actually happened in Jonah's case. See Jonah 4.

In statistical terms, Jonah was the most successful prophet-evangelist in the Old Testament era: a three-day "city-wide crusade" brought 120,000 people to repentance, including the king and the government. Yet the evangelist himself was completely out of sync with the heart of God. Even his own experience of the astonishing grace of God to a determined sinner failed to soften him.

In a sense you can understand him. After all, Assyria, like Nazi Germany, was guilty of the most horrendous cruelty, not least to his own nation. It was not easy to feel compassion for such evil people, but that is what his calling as a man of God required. If he was called to share in God's work he must also share God's heart. That is where the problem lay. For Jonah, patriotic feelings were stronger than prophetic fidelity. He achieved professional success but failed to please God. The truth is that we, too, can be "successful" in our particular sphere of life and ministry and yet fail to please God who *"looks not on the outward appearance but on the heart"*.

It is possible to take a strong stand on moral issues such as adultery, abortion, homosexuality and the like, but to do so in a harsh, condemning spirit that is foreign to the compassion of Christ and fails to seek to minister to the fallen. It is possible to exercise "dynamic" leadership with a hardness of heart that is so unlike *"the meekness and gentleness of Christ"* (2 Corinthians 10:1); a leadership that manages rather than ministers, and bruises rather than blesses.

It is possible vociferously to *"defend the Faith"* and thunder against the perceived errors of others while at the same time failing to realise *"what kind of spirit you are of"* (Luke 9:53-55). When such so-called "righteous anger" is not scrupulously careful with the facts and then resorts to hurling personal abuse in the aggressive manner of some contemporary self-appointed "guardians of the truth" it is foreign to the spirit of him who wept when pronouncing judgment (Luke 19:41f.).

It is possible to preach the Gospel with great fervour and apparently achieve great success, but to do so from an ambitious and competitive spirit which is totally at odds with the compelling love of Christ which moved Paul (Philippians 1:15-17; cf. 2 Corinthians 5:14, 15).

It is possible to be a highly accomplished worship leader, play an instrument skillfully, or simply join in congregational singing enthusiastically with upraised hands, and yet live in such a way that makes God wince over the awful spiritual discords we produce (Matthew 15:8, 9). Success isn't everything. Above all else, God looks for heart beating in rhythm with his own. Jonah had to learn that. So do we!

## *Paul's Philosophy of Ministry*

He looked at me quizzically. "Philosophy of ministry, what on earth are you talking about?"

"Well, you know," I stammered.

"No! I don't know," he almost shouted. "Why must you use such big words? Why don't you say what you mean?"

I tried again, "Paul, 'philosophy of ministry' simply means the way you fulfil your ministry and run your church."

He looked at me with disdain. "Then why on earth didn't you say so? Why do you have to use posh words like…?" – his voice trailed away as if he didn't want to repeat the offending words.

"I'm sorry," I said, "it's the modern way of putting things. We never use simple words when more complicated ones are available. It sounds more impressive that way."

He shot me with another withering look. "Exactly what I said to the Galatians about those Judaisers – wanting to make a fair show in the flesh. Why do you have a philosophy of ministry? Why can't you just have a ministry?"

"But Paul, you taught principles of ministry in your letters you know."

He snorted derisively.

"There you go again. Now it's principles of ministry. Why must you always want to make it so technical? Look here, what the Spirit inspired me to write were some personal letters to the churches God enabled me to found. I never sat down and tried to write an official manual on church structures. For instance, I mentioned in one letter, to the Ephesians, about various special ministries God has set in the church – and what do you people do? You insist on creating a 'Five-fold Ministry' structure out of what was a fairly general observation. I wasn't making a definitive theological statement; I was simply remarking on God's gracious provision for the church through the ages."

"I'm sorry, Paul, I hadn't thought of it like that. But then what you wrote was none other than the Word of God. It carries supreme authority."

"That's just the point," he said. "The fact is, that God is often not so precise as you moderns want him to be. You are always looking for exact statements – about the Trinity for example – and they're not there. You want blueprints for church structures and they're not there either. People want detailed prophetic projections, closely defined statements about all kinds of things, but God has chosen to be more flexible than religious people like." He studied me closely. "The trouble with you moderns is that you're so taken up with structures and methods of doing things. You're more concerned with how things look; you're always wanting to be seen to be clever and successful. You can use this complicated 'in' language, the language of the business world, the language of psychology and media. You 'read' into what I and others wrote, things that aren't really there. You quote us to give your theories 'biblical' respectability and most of the time you make simple things so complicated. Why don't you call a 'spade a spade'? This posh language of yours is the verbal coinage of religious inflation; it's the megabucks of a devalued currency."

After such an outburst I was afraid to look at him, but suddenly he had laid a gentle hand on my shoulder. "Now I know how Peter felt when you 'withstood him to his face' in Antioch," I said. A smile quivered round his lips. "Come," he said almost playfully, "I'll show you my…hmmm… philosophy of ministry!" We sat down and he put his arm around my shoulders.

"Look," he said, "it all began when Christ laid his hand on me. I was the 'chief of sinners,' I was a blasphemer, a persecutor and a violent man, and I was thundering down the Damascus road with murder in my heart, on my way to arrest the Christians, when I was arrested myself. Christ laid his hands on me… did even more, embraced me in astonishing love. That love was shed abroad in my heart and now it 'constrains me.'"

He paused and looked at me intently. "Do you know what I meant when I said 'constrains?'"

"That's in 2 Corinthians 5:14, King James Version," I said. He shook his head playfully. "You and your chapters and verses! I wrote letters, not theological textbooks. No, I chose my words carefully – really it was the Holy Spirit who taught me what to say – and what I wanted to convey by that word 'constrains' was the idea of tremendous pressure, like being squeezed between two moving walls and being urged forward. This love of Christ exerts such a pressure on me that I find myself carried along by it. My ministry, my attitude to people, my whole life is a love response. As my friend John would say, *'We love because he first loved us.'*"

He began to walk up and down, as if the momentum of the love of Christ was working through his whole being. "When you begin to grasp how wide and long, and high and deep is the love of Christ," he said, "you can't do enough for him and you just want to let everyone within range know about that love. Of course you try to use the best method of doing things, but it is more than a matter of techniques, it's a passion for Christ."

"I can see that," I said, "but Paul, you had a brilliant academic training under Gamaliel in Jerusalem. You had a Master's degree in Old Testament theology; you had advantages that most of us never had. And the way you went about things was brilliant. I mean, it was so well organized and efficient."

He stopped pacing and stood in front of me. "I'm not denying the importance of academics, training and developing skills of ministry, but what concerns me is the way in which people put more confidence in those things than in the real spiritual dynamics. Listen, when I first went to Corinth I had already learned that *'the world by wisdom does not know God.'* What they needed was not more philosophy but the Gospel of the Cross. So what I offered them was not an exercise in 'state of the art' communication skills, rather I came *'not with eloquence or superior wisdom... I resolved to know nothing... except Jesus Christ and him crucified. I came in weakness and trembling. My message and my preaching were not with wise and persuasive words, but with a demonstration of the Spirit's power.'"*

"I accept that," I said, "but you did have well developed methods. I mean, you usually went for the cities and then you seemed to follow a definite pattern... Take Athens for instance: First the synagogue, then the market place, then the meeting of the philosophers."

He sighed. "There you go again, trying to build a structure of missionary policy out of a few references from the book of Acts. I've told you, I was driven by the overwhelming love of Christ, but I had no explicit programme. My evangelistic ministry began when the Holy Spirit selected Barnabas and me at the prayer meeting in Antioch. My ministry is the not the result of managerial skills; I followed the promptings of the Holy Spirit. When he said 'Go!' I went, when he said 'Don't go there,' I did as I was told."

"Oh yes," I said. "Like Luke described your movements in Acts chapter 16 verse..." I didn't finish because he was staring at me again.

Another thought struck me. "Paul, it isn't easy to conduct your ministry in that way. I mean, it's so easy to say you've 'heard from God,' when really it's just your own ideas and enthusiasms floating to the surface. I know a lot of people who are always claiming..."

He took me by the arm and led me in his pacing. "Now you're either led by the Spirit or you fall back on human substitutes and quite honestly, the human substitutes are much more – what's the modern term, 'user friendly' than the real thing. Do you want to know the real 'philosophy of my ministry'? I'll tell you." He stopped and released his hold on me. His eyes had a far away look and his face was suffused with inspired intensity. His voice trembled with emotion as the words came pouring out: *"As servants of God we commend ourselves in every way, in great endurance, in troubles, hardships, and distress, in beatings, imprisonments and riots, in hard work, sleepless nights and hunger, in purity, understanding, patience and kindness, in the Holy Spirit and in sincere love, in truthful speech and in the power of God, with weapons of righteousness in the right hand and in the left, through glory and dishonour, bad report and good report, as genuine, yet regarded as imposters, known yet regarded as unknown, dying, and behold we live on, beaten, and yet not killed, sorrowful, yet always rejoicing, poor, yet making many rich, having nothing, yet possessing everything."*

"That makes me and my philosophy of ministry look pretty poor," I murmured. He smiled and again laid his hand on my shoulder. "Don't be discouraged by trying to measure yourself against other people and their ministries. Look to Christ! Don't be so taken up with the mechanics of 'Christian service' that you lose sight of Jesus himself. The world is taken up with outward appearance, and too many Christians succumb to the spirit of the age. Look at their advertising, 'The biggest since'... 'the fastest growing'... 'the greatest'... 'the most significant'... Why do they do it? What are they trying to prove? It's the way of the world. Remember what the Lord Jesus said, *'the kingdom of God does not come with observation'*, or as one of your modern translations puts it, *'with outward show!'"*

I shifted uneasily, then, in the comfortable stillness I heard his fierce whisper as he drove his fist into the palm of his hand, *"God forbid that I should boast, save in the Cross of our Lord Jesus Christ, by whom the world is crucified unto me, and I unto the world."*

## The Church and "Yoof" Culture

On a cold February morning in 1554, a slender, auburn-haired girl of 16 stood trembling on the scaffold in the Tower of London. Facing her was the black-clad executioner and the wooden block on which she was about to lay her young head. Jane Grey was a remarkable teenager. Competent in several languages, including Latin and Greek, she was also passionate in her evangelical faith. But she was a pawn in a desperate game of political chess. Forced against her will to become queen, she "reigned" for only nine days before Mary I replaced her. Shortly afterwards, Mary signed her death warrant.

Lady Jane Grey could have escaped death had she been willing to deny her Protestant faith. They tried nearly everything, even to her last moments, to make her recant; but she refused to deny her faith in the sole sufficiency of Jesus Christ and his atoning blood. Eventually the axe blade flashed in the sullen winter light and another young martyr went to a coronation more glorious than the one self-serving men had planned for her.

On a terrifying day in 2003 in Nigeria, Malam Kasimu, uncle and guardian of 15-year-old Salamantu Hassan, vented his rage over her conversion to Christ: "If you were my daughter," he shouted, "I would have slaughtered you, killed you here, you bastard infidel, for turning away from Islam." He threw her out with nowhere to go but the street.

Hassan had received Christ through the witness of another Christian, but it was not long before her aunt and uncle learned of her faith and tried to force her into embracing Islam. They beat her and deprived her of food for days, and forced her to attend their rituals. She stood firm in her faith in Christ, however, and finally she was deprived of all her possessions and driven out. Eventually, Christian friends came to her aid; today she is a student at a College of Education in Akwanga.

Like Jane Grey, Hassan has stood firm: "I have found true salvation in Jesus, the right way to God," she says. "Never will I go back."
Separated by 450 years of history, these two teenagers are shining examples of young people who have stood for Christ in the midst of appalling opposition. There are uncounted multitudes of others. It is said that there have been more martyrs for Christ in the last decades than there have been through the history of the Church, and many of them are young people who have chosen to be "faithful unto death."

All over the world, teenagers join older people in facing persecution, imprisonment and death for Christ's sake. They are the elite troops of the church militant.

Now take a look at the young people in your church. They may not dress to your liking, and sometimes they could do with being a bit more "reverent", at least as far as "normal" standards go – whatever they may be. But look beyond the clothes and hairstyles; consider the homes from which some of them come; consider the pressures to which they are subjected through the media with its godless materialism and impudent sensuality; ponder the daily battle they fight against the aggressive attitudes of fellow students and colleagues at work. I speak as one who faced "the opposition of sinful men" in RAF barrack rooms, and remember that to live out the Christian life in a hostile world is a call to walk the "Calvary road".

At the present time in our own country, but for how long we do not know, teenagers are not called upon to die for Christ, but they do face a costly choice between being loyal to Christ, for the faith, and for the values of purity and integrity, or of compromising with the hostile, sneering world of the ungodly. They need our prayers, our personal encouragement and rather more patience than we sometimes give them.

Who knows, some of them may be destined for martyrdom in the ultimate sense of the word.

## You Don't Need Rocket Science, In Order to Please God

It lay among the autumn leaves, blackened and forlorn. A passing dog sniffed at it momentarily and trotted away. No one else gave it even a glance. Yet hours before it had soared into the November night, accompanied by the "oohs" and "aahs" of a delighted crowd, and finally exploded into a crackling cascade of multi-coloured stars. Now it lay forgotten by the wayside, a sad symbol of "burnout" and of the transience of so much that the world admires as spectacular and successful. As the psalmist declared, *"As for man, his days are like grass, he flourishes like a flower of the field; the wind blows over it and it is gone, and its place remembers it no more"* (Psalm 103:15, 16; cf. Isaiah 40:6-8).

Flying into East Midlands airport one Guy Fawkes night some time ago, one could see fireworks exploding below. From the ground they were no doubt drawing gasps of admiration as they burst into a brilliant display that lit the night sky, but from thousands of feet above they appeared no more than miniscule flashes of light soon swallowed up in the prevailing darkness. Once again they were a reminder of the fact that what, from the human point of view, is most impressive is often, from God's perspective, far less so. In the words of Isaiah, *"As the heavens are higher than the earth, so are my ways higher than your ways and my thoughts than your thoughts"* (Isaiah 55:9). In other words, to use an already overworked piece of modern jargon, pleasing God is not a matter of rocket science.

In the world of pyrotechnics, rocket science means many hours of planning and the expenditure of huge sums of money in creating what can be admittedly beautiful but of frustratingly brief duration. As you watch the brilliant colours drift away into thin grey smoke you find yourself asking, "Was it really worth it?"

In the politico/scientific world, rocket science produces spectacular achievements in space travel and exploration, giving power to politicians and prestige to scientists; but viewing the huge costs in terms of time, effort and money involved, one is again forced to wonder whether, against the overwhelming needs of a hungry, disease-ridden, war-torn planet, it is really justified. The story of the tower of Babel (Genesis 11) is a warning that humankind's search for globalised solidarity and prestigious technological achievement do not always meet with divine approval.

There are times when the modern church needs to ask equally searching questions about itself. Reading the promotional literature that is published in some places and searching the websites of some churches and organisations, one gets the feeling that they have imbibed the spirit of the age in a quest for an upmarket image. While they have abandoned the somewhat archaic "language of Zion", in many cases they have replaced it with the "language of Babylon" – the "spin" of the advertising agent. Everything is made to sound so sophisticated, so "cutting edge", so "contemporary", so self-assured, and sometimes so complicated that it seems far different from the self-effacing simplicity of Jesus (Matthew 11:29). Sometimes one wonders about the real, long-term spiritual value of it all, and, more importantly, what he makes of it. He was certainly not impressed by the "website" of the church at Laodicea (Revelation 3:17).

To people who were keen to "make a good show of things", Micah (6:6-8) pointed out that God was not overly impressed by such displays. What will really please God? he asked. Great acts of sacrificial service? The achievements of outstanding religious enterprise? The rocket science of sophisticated techniques of ministry and worship? No! *What does the Lord require of you? To act justly, and to love mercy, and to walk humbly with your God.* Like Paul (1 Corinthians 13:1-3), Micah knew that God is not impressed by the fireworks of enthusiastic human endeavour, but looks for the fire of a sacred love that seeks him with genuine passion for himself and his glory.

## Don't Let the World Set the Agenda

The Bible is sometimes an uncomfortable book. You read it as part of your devotions, quietly enjoying its stories and being blessed by its inspired words, and then, suddenly, it points its finger at you!

It happened to me recently. Reading through the second book of Kings, I was fascinated by the story of King Ahaz's visit to Damascus for an "international summit" with the Assyrian king, Tiglath-Pileser (2 Kings 16). The location and the occasion sounded so much like the politics of our own day — it was a "good read"!

What followed was even more interesting: in Damascus, Ahaz saw a pagan altar which so impressed him that he had drawings of it sent to Jerusalem, with orders for a replica of it to be made in order to replace Solomon's great altar in the Temple. That set me thinking: How could Ahaz replace a Holy Spirit-designed altar (see 1 Chronicles 28:11-19) with a pagan one? Surely, that was "copying the world".

It was at that point that the Bible pointed its finger at me! It seemed to say, "Isn't the modern church in danger of doing the same kind of thing? Isn't much of her life influenced by 'contemporary culture', causing her to adjust her theology, her methods and her lifestyle in order to meet the challenge of the present age?"

Take, for instance, the "altar" of the cross. In some quarters of evangelical thinking, the old biblical altar of substitutionary atonement has been replaced with a new one which copies the more attractive designs created by post-modern "insights". The uncompromising lines of the old altar, with its emphasis on the sinfulness of sin, the unutterable holiness of God, the certainty of judgement and the need for propitiation and repentance, have been replaced by the softer, more rounded shape of the new one. This new altar manages to remove some aspects of the "offence of the cross" by offering a revised version of Christ's atonement which is more acceptable to modern sensibilities.

The word "contemporary" is a powerful one; it affects the way we "do church", the way we worship, the way we communicate the Gospel, the way we counsel people, and the values that determine our lifestyle. The slogan, "The Church must move with the times", is equally powerful; but while it contains elements of truth, it also contains subtle seeds of compromise.

The Church is called to challenge the culture, not conform to it. That is why Paul says, *"Do not conform any longer to the pattern of this world"* (Romans 12:2); and why John writes, *"Do not love the world or anything in the world... For everything in the world — the cravings of sinful people, the lust of their eyes and their boasting about what they have and do — comes not from the Father..."* (1 John 2:15-16). In other words, don't let the world set the agenda.

When preaching replaces careful exposition of the Word of God with popular sound bites (2 Timothy 4:2-4)... when worship is more like a rock concert than the robust, God-centred praise of the Psalms and Revelation... when counselling methods are more influenced by some of the dubious techniques of popular psychology than by biblical principles... when leadership styles seem to turn pastors into business managers rather than Spirit-anointed ministers... when churches seem more like religious factories urgently working to meet "customer demand" rather than seeking to be what Jesus said it should be – *"my Father's house, a house of prayer"*... and when our personal values reflect the aspirations of the consumer society in which we live rather than seeking first the kingdom of God – then we have allowed the world to set the agenda.

If the above descriptions match our experience, then we have replaced the Spirit-designed, biblical altar for a pagan one, and we will fare no better than Ahaz. Our "road to Damascus" has led us in the wrong direction and we had better turn back, for *"anyone who chooses to be a friend of the world becomes an enemy of God"* (James 4:4).

Perhaps we need to have a fresh look at our "altars".

## Let the Bible do the Talking

In the early days of the space race, when the Russians had launched their small, round Sputniks into orbit, someone referred to the famous, eloquent and rotund Welsh politician, Aneurin Bevan, as "a small, spherical object going round in ever-decreasing circles, emitting strange noises!"

That story evoked the memory of a preacher I once heard. He had announced his text and I was immediately riveted: *"He has also set eternity in the hearts of men"* (Ecclesiastes 3:11). Here was an opportunity to explore little known biblical territory and I eagerly waited for the expedition to start. Sadly, it never happened. The text was merely a pretext, a launching pad for the preacher's flight into a personal orbit that merely went round in circles. We heard personal reminiscences and general observations on spiritual life, but we never did learn what eternity in people's hearts really meant. We felt cheated.

That in turn reminds me of listening to a galaxy of Pentecostal/Charismatic preachers from all over the world at a certain conference. Night after night, famous speakers stood behind the podium, or, more frequently, ranged across the platform like lions on the prowl. But of all those messages, I only remember the one on Joshua 1 preached by Jack Hayford – because he alone actually expounded the Word of God.

The truth is that, homiletical gymnastics and presentational fireworks may impress at the time, but their impact is soon lost – they sparkle and crackle for a few moments but fall to earth like spent rockets. Witticisms wilt, histrionics fade, performance ministry evaporates, but *"the Word of the Lord remains for ever"* (1 Peter 1:25 ESV). That is why Paul says, *"Preach the Word"* (2 Timothy 4:2).

The danger for us preachers is that we can easily preach from the Word without actually preaching the Word. We use the Bible as a useful starting point and quote from it to give authority to what we are saying, but often we do not let the Bible do the talking. Like experienced tailors, we shape the Word to fit our personal "insights" instead of allowing it to shape us, our thinking, and our preaching. So the question for preachers is: "What is the Bible actually saying?" not, "What do I think it is saying?" or "How can I find texts to support my personal views?"

Paul warns us about *"distorting the Word of God"* (2 Corinthians 4:2) and urges Timothy – and us – to handle the Word of God correctly (2 Timothy 2:15). That will take time, prayer, diligent study, openness to the Holy Spirit, integrity, and a willingness to come to uncomfortable conclusions sometimes. Like Jeremiah, we need to be able to say, *"You know what came out of my lips; it was before your face"* (Jeremiah 17:16 ESV).

The people in our congregations must also let the Bible do the talking. For one thing, they need to start reading it! A Bible Society survey has revealed that, on average, only ten people in a congregation of 50 read the Bible every day, and 30% don't read it at all between Sundays. With so much biblical anorexia among us, it is little wonder so many churches are so feeble. Too many Christians feed themselves on a high calorie diet of religious television – like highly-salted canned soup of varying nutritional value – instead of on the pure milk and strong meat of the Word of God.

It is not only a return to Bible reading that we need, however, but also a return to Bible behaving. We need to let the Bible do the talking – to listen to what it is actually saying, and start doing what it says. Only then will we stop going round in circles like spiritual "Sputniks", going nowhere and getting weaker. Only then will the sounds we utter in ministry, worship and fellowship be meaningful.

## In a Fractured World, Whatever Happens – Stay Connected

On January 21st, 1930, King George V was to give an address to the London Arms Conference. For the first time his voice was to be heard throughout the world via a radio broadcast.

Suddenly, disaster struck. A few minutes before the speech was due, a member of staff at America's CBS studio tripped over a cable and broke it. In desperation, Harold Vivian, the chief control operator, grasped one end of the broken cable in his right hand and the other end in his left hand, restoring the circuit. Two hundred and fifty volts of electricity surged through his arms and body, but he refused to let go and consequently the king's message reached its American audience.

It's not difficult to see the thrust of that story. We live in a world which is disconnected from its Maker – its sins have separated it from a holy God. The tragic picture of Adam and Eve slowly walking hand in hand out of Paradise into an unknown future, in a world suffering the after-shock of their sin, is the symbol of the costly consequences of human rebellion against God and the alienation it brings.

Moreover, there is no man-made way back. The ill-fated attempt to reach heaven with the tower of Babel is likewise a symbol of the futility of every human attempt to reach the lost horizon. Genesis 11:1-9 reveals that the politics of "globalization", the latest developments in technology, and the pride-driven quest for celebrity status cannot enable mankind to reach for the skies. As the apostle John puts it, *"Everything in the world – the cravings of sinful man, the lust of his eyes and the boasting of what he has and does – comes not from the Father but from the world..."* (1 John 2:16), a world with a limited "sell-by date".

Somehow, someone, somewhere, has got to restore the broken connection. There lies the glory of the Incarnation – the atoning death and triumphant resurrection of the Lord Jesus Christ. In him alone the broken connection between a holy God and a fallen race is restored; in him alone the voice of God is clearly heard; in him alone the high-voltage surge of the power of God flows in saving grace into a world deafened and paralysed by sin. He *"has destroyed the barrier, the dividing wall of hostility... thus making peace, and... reconciling both of them (Jews and Gentiles) to God through the cross, by which he put to death their hostility. He came and preached peace..."* (Ephesians 2:14-17). Sadly, too many people trip over cables in the place where the voice of the King should be transmitted to the world – the "Christian Broadcasting Service" of the local church and its members.

The breakdown in communication is two-fold. Far too many church members are failing to connect with the essential flow of the power of God through the fullness of the Holy Spirit. They seem to imagine they can get by with a minimal level of dependence on the Spirit's power and so they give little time to seeking his enabling. They have forgotten that Acts 1:8 is not simply a nice promise but an irreducible requirement which demands we take it seriously, or else...

The other breakdown lies in the failure of many Christians to connect with the world that needs to hear and see and feel the flow of God's transforming grace. We need to "complete the circuit" between the power of God and the desperate need of the people around us. It is time to grasp the hands of needy sinners with the message of the Gospel and through meaningful relationships allow the power of the Word and the Spirit to flow through us.

This means more than a nod at the neighbours; it means taking time and real effort to build bridges across the barriers that divide us from the people among whom we live and move and have our being.

People need to hear the King's voice. We must stay connected – with him and them.

## Don't Keep Jesus Waiting in the Porch, "Enjoy a Candlelit Dinner" with Him!

Under the title, "How to buy gold when you're broke" John Piper preached a sermon on Christ's message to the church in Laodicea (Revelation 3:14-22) in which he made the following thought-provoking statement: "Christ did not die to redeem a bride who would keep him in the porch while she watched television in the den. His will for the church is that we open all the doors of our life. He wants to join you in the dining room, spread out a meal for you, eat and talk with you. The opposite of lukewarmness is the fervour you experience when you enjoy a candle-lit dinner with Jesus Christ in the innermost part of your life."

Paul's words to the Ephesians (3:17) resonate with the same sense of intimacy with Christ. As Kenneth S Wuest renders them in his *Expanded Ttranslation,* "That the Christ may finally settle down and feel completely at home in your hearts through faith". It is important to note that the one who seeks this intimacy with us is not simply Jesus, but "The Christ": The divinely anointed Messiah, coming to us as the great prophet who speaks with absolute authority, the Priest through whom alone sinful people have access to a holy God, and the King upon whose shoulders the destiny of the universe rests. To Laodicea, he came as *"The Amen* (the final word,) *the faithful and true witness, the ruler of God's creation."* Thus for them to keep him "in the porch", was an unspeakable affront and a spiritual blunder of catastrophic proportions. It led to bankruptcy. In the same way, for us tacitly to marginalise him from the centre of our church or personal life, the place where decisions are made, values determined, and plans initiated is unthinkable – but it happens! We too often leave him "in the porch" while we get on with things. That's why we are so ineffectual.

138

"Is there anything you don't like?" asked my hostess prior to a recent visit. Laughingly, I replied, "Tripe!" But I was thankful for her kindly concern for my happiness while in her home. That is the kind of question we need to ask Jesus: "Lord is there anything you don't like about our church and personal lives?" After all, we may be pleased about things, but is he? Laodicea thought they were a most successful church and *"had need of nothing"*, but Jesus didn't see it that way at all. In his eyes, they were bankrupt, and to him the spiritual "menu" they served up was revolting (Revelation 3: 16). He called for radical change.

If Christ is to feel completely at home, we must make sure that things are congenial to him. He will certainly feel ill at ease in a church or life that is unclean or in which there is an unloving atmosphere. We need to heed Paul's advice in Ephesians 3: 10 and *"find out what pleases the Lord"*. He spells this out in Romans 12:1-2: a sacrificial lifestyle which offers *"spiritual worship"* and is able to *"test and approve what God's will is"* and won't compromise with the world is pleasing to him (cf. Hebrews 13: 15-16). So he urges the Colossians (1:10-12) to *"live a life worthy of the Lord and to please him in every way, bearing fruit in every good work, growing in the knowledge of God, being strengthened with all power... and joyfully giving thanks to the Father..."* Pleasing God also means obeying parents (Colossians 3: 20) and the proper care of older family members (1 Timothy 5: 4). It touches every area of life and conduct.

In spite of its flawed condition, Jesus still wanted an intimate relationship with Laodicea, hence his call, "Listen to me and open the door". We, too, must hear *"what the Spirit is saying"* and respond to his voice. D H Lawrence wrote many controversial books, but he also wrote a poem entitled *Pax* which, surprisingly, sums it all up:

> *Finding the presence of the living God*
> *Like a great assurance*
> *A deep calm in the heart*

*A presence*
*As of the master sitting at the board*
*In his own and greater being*
*In the house of life*

When "Jesus himself draws near" and gains access to the centre of our church and personal life, transforming things take place!

# Living in Changing Times

# *Reflections*

# When "Aunty" tells lies, the rest of the family had better watch their step!

**N**early everyone has one. They come in all shapes and sizes. Some are plump and cuddly; some are thin and seem a bit austere (though there's a smile round the edges of pursed lips); some have deep laughter lines etched on their faces; some seem dreary; some are just funny – but they all have one thing in common: they're favourite aunts, the one person in the mixed allsorts of family members you know you can trust. When no one else seems to understand, you know that "aunty" will provide a listening ear and a comforting arm. Like my Aunty Betty, of blessed memory, who, with a conspiratorial chuckle, used to give me condensed milk on bread and butter for my tea!

Favourite aunts are wonderful people, but if they should do something wrong it feels as if the world will come to an end. That, it seems, has happened to the BBC in recent times. Affectionately known to so many people as "Aunty", the institution that seemed to be the epitome of rectitude and unbiased reporting has been caught out telling lies. First, a series of badly organised competitions; then, horror of horrors, a wrongly edited clip that suggested the Queen had lost her "cool"! No wonder Jeremy Paxman, John Humphries and friends have been sent on an "honesty" course!

We're not surprised when newspapers twist stories to sell more copies, or that politicians are "economical with the truth", or that big business is embroiled with fraud, or that sportsmen cheat, but when our favourite aunt is caught out doing the same we feel betrayed: *"Truth has stumbled in the public squares"* (Isaiah 54:19, ESV).

The betrayal of trust undermines the foundations of life – in marriage, friendship, politics, business, and most of all in spiritual life. When the Church "edits" the biblical script in order to make doctrine more palatable to modern thinking, and when modern Christians cut the

143

cloth of their moral standards to follow the fashions of contemporary culture they are betraying their trust as those called to be salt and light in a fallen world. What is more, the world will see through our feeble attempt at compromise, and God hates it (James 4:4).

Against a background of stormy waves, treacherous winds and theological pirates on the high seas, Paul urges the church in Ephesus to steer a straight course by *"speaking the truth in love"* (Ephesians 4:14-16). Only thus can they reach their destiny in God.

*"Speaking the truth in love"* certainly means being true to the great doctrines of the faith, but it also means integrity in every area of life (see v. 25f.). It means honesty in preaching, in leadership, in handling money, as well as in personal relationships. The warm embrace in the Sunday morning "fellowship time" is meaningless if, during Sunday lunch, by means of critical comments the "embraced" become the "disgraced". We only truly worship *"in Spirit and in truth"* when we are lovingly honest.

In an age when moral and spiritual dishonesty breed distrust and, even worse, cynicism, the church must prove itself by its faithfulness in doctrine and high standards of public behaviour to be the one group of people in the world who can be trusted.

The church will never be the world's "favourite aunty", but she must not allow herself to become a legitimate "Aunt Sally" because she says and does things that deserve the scorn of the ungodly. At all costs we must be true to Christ (Matthew 5:10-12).

## *You Are What You Eat*

In the late 1960s, more "advanced" Christians spoke with a certain dismissive air about the "hymn-prayer-hymn-Bible reading sandwich" that provided the spiritual diet of most evangelical and Pentecostal churches in layers of a fairly predictable order of service. The upmarket ones replaced this with what one is tempted to call a "chorus soup", in which 57 varieties of new songs, some containing a strange mixture of theological ingredients, were made available to the spiritually hungry in an unending flow of "singspiration".

Life has moved on. Like its counterpart in the world of celebrity chefs, the modern church, with unparalleled access to multi-media resources, is able to provide an exotic cuisine of spiritual fare. We can all dine out at expensive restaurants called conferences, Bible weeks and seminars, or we can order "room service" which will bring an amazing choice of menus into our own homes through books, DVDs, CDs, the Internet and religious TV. And, of course, there is always "Sunday lunch" at our "local"!

The problem with all this abundance is: how healthy is it? Will it produce charismatic cholesterol? Will it encourage spiritual obesity? Will it increase our intake of moral fatty acids? Will it induce a greater risk of heart disease? Or will it create a generation of spiritual anorexics?

Many years ago, one of our conferences was enlivened by a gifted preacher whose charm, wit, humour, mastery of words and theatrical skill were outstanding (older readers should not try to guess his identity!). We loved every minute of it, but on reflection one realised it was like a lemon meringue pie – delicious for a treat, but not the stuff you could live on through a working week. Plain, home-made meals would be much more satisfying, and in the end more healthy.

You don't have to be a spiritual foodie to know that what the mind and heart feed on will have a profound effect on the kind of Christian you become. That is why New Testament writers emphasise the importance of *"pure spiritual milk"* (1 Peter 2:2) and *"solid food"* (1Corinthians 3:1, 2; Hebrews 5:12-14). Interestingly, the writer of Hebrews, after four tightly packed chapters which will stretch most modern readers, complains that his readers are not mature enough to tackle a steak! Sadly, too, many church members are still crying for milk and many of them for condensed milk at that! Easily digested spiritual snacks may give temporary satisfaction but they do not provide the all-important proteins and vitamins the Holy Spirit desires to impart as he explores and explains *"the deep things of God"* (1 Corinthians 2:6-16). It is only as we absorb and inwardly digest those deep things that we are able to *"grow in grace and the knowledge of our Lord Jesus Christ"* (1 Peter 3:18).

That doesn't mean that solid teaching has to be humourless or boring; it does mean that we are prepared to do some real thinking, to grapple with challenging truths and seek to understand the glorious mysteries of Christian doctrine so that we can give a reason for the faith we say we believe and manifest the beauty of full-grown Christian manhood and womanhood. After all, that's one of the main reasons the Holy Spirit has come – John 14:26; 16:13-15.

The danger is that we have so much access to such a variety of spiritual food (some of it junk) that some preachers are serving up "convenience food" obtained from the Internet supermarket instead of devoting themselves to prayer and the Word of God in true apostolic ministry (Acts 6:2-4). And many Christians are existing unhealthily on "takeaways" found on the *God Channel* and other easy-to-prepare substitutes for a deep personal encounter with God instead of coming to the Word of God for themselves, praying into it, thinking it through and then doing what it says.

Perhaps that's why some Christians are so anaemic and lethargic. They need to get back on to a proper Word-based diet (Colossians 3:16) and reach for their "trainers" (1 Timothy 4:7, 8).

## *Watch Your Body Language*

**"O**ur body is a machine for living" (Leo Tolstoy, *War and Peace*).

"Your body is a blank canvas – we'll make it a work of art" (sign in a hairdresser's window).

"My body is not a temple, it's a funfair!" (slogan on a T-shirt in an Oxford shop).

*"Do you not know that your body is a temple of the Holy Spirit"* (1Corinthians 6:19).

So what is it? A machine, a piece of artwork, a funfair, or a temple? The question is important, because as you see it so you will treat it, and how you treat it will determine what it says about you, and what will happen to it in the end.

In one sense Tolstoy was right. The human body is a marvellous piece of machinery designed for human beings to explore what life is all about. No wonder the psalmist exclaimed, *"I am fearfully and wonderfully made"* (139:14) as he thought about the mystery of his birth – *"knit together in my mother's womb"* (v 13). The superbly designed mechanism of the body, its faculties, organs, bone structure, nervous system and tissues, enables humankind to achieve astonishing feats of endurance and creative attainment, at the same time possessing remarkable powers of self-renewal.

"What a piece of work is man!" cried Shakespeare. "…how infinite in faculties! in form and moving, how express and admirable!" (*Hamlet* II:ii). He was right, but the body is more than a machine.

Even well-designed machines can be improved on – at least, that is what the beauticians believe. Maybe they're right. A glance in the mirror, for most of us, will probably confirm it. No wonder James says we are quick to forget what we see (James 1:24), though he meant it spiritually. The truth is that the body is not merely an "empty canvas", it is a damaged masterpiece made in the image of its Creator but vandalised by sin, and no amount of fresh paint can remove the damage. We need something more than cosmetics, we need *"the unfading beauty of a gentle and quiet spirit, which is of great worth in God's sight"* (1 Peter 3:3, 4) and which God's Spirit alone can create in us.

With their bright lights and burgers, candy floss and carousels, side-shows and rollercoasters, funfairs provide plenty of thrills and spills, but when the music stops and the lights dim, all you've done is go round in circles, eating unhealthy food and experiencing stomach-lurching ups and downs. To treat our bodies as nothing more than playthings is to desecrate something designed for a purpose much more important than that.

The people to whom Paul wrote in 1 Corinthians 6 knew all about temples. Shrines to a multiplicity of gods were everywhere, but in their pagan lifestyle their own bodies had become like ruined temples dedicated to the gods of power, wealth, sex and drink (see vv 9-10). Then the divine bulldozers and builders came on site (vv 11-20), and the work of the regeneration of these derelict moral slums began through the power of the Gospel.

It's worth noting that Paul calls the body – not just the soul or spirit – the temple of the Holy Spirit. In other words, all that we are physically, as well as spiritually, intellectually and emotionally, has been purchased by the blood of Christ with a view to its becoming a holy place in which God dwells and reveals his glory. That invests our bodies with a sacredness which demands that we care for them and use them reverently and pre-eminently for him. After all, his plans for them reach into eternity (Romans 8:23; 1 Corinthians 15:51-57; Philippians 3:20, 21).

## *How are your Metatarsals?*

It is probably true that, until the end of April 2006, very few people knew what or where the metatarsals were. Newspaper columnist Jim White says that, until David Beckham broke his, he thought Metatarsals were galactic villains from some Dan Dare fantasy.

Now, thanks to Man United star Wayne Rooney, everybody knows that they are a vital part of the foot. The sight of him rolling over in anguish, clutching his foot, made the nation gasp in horror.

By the time you are reading this Rooney's and England's fate in the 2006 World Cup will be known; but it is salutary to realise that it will all have depended on a few inches of bone in a Liverpudlian foot. It helps you to understand why Paul said, *"The head cannot say to the feet, 'I don't need you'."* It also adds a modern touch to Solomon's advice: *"Guard your steps when you go to the house of God"* (Ecclesiastes 5:1). The metatarsals of the Spirit are very important but easily damaged.

Interestingly enough, many sports writers blame the damage to footballers' feet on the design of their boots. Apparently they are designed, like many other things these days, for speed rather than security – as a "fashion statement" rather than for stability. All of which makes Ephesians 6:15 very relevant: *"With your feet fitted with the readiness that comes from the gospel of peace."* Granted, the picture is a military one, but the implications are plain: stability as well as mobility depend upon the right footwear.

John Stott, in his commentary on Ephesians, quotes Marcus Barth's description of the legionaries' footwear as being made of strong leather, and having studded soles which gave him mobility as well as a strong footing in difficult terrain. He goes on to suggest that the Christian's "boots" may refer to the actual message of the Gospel which gives him peace, freedom and security in a hostile world. Or it may refer to the light-footed eagerness with which he is determined to take the Gospel into that needy world. Either way, he must be properly equipped if he is to play his part in spiritual warfare and engage in effective evangelism. Isaiah says feet like that are *"beautiful"* (52:7) because they are the feet of "a messenger with a spring in his step" bringing good news.

In the midst of a "worst case scenario" where, Habakkuk says, *"decay crept into my bones, and my legs trembled,"* he could still say, *"He makes my feet like the feet of a deer, he enables me to go on the heights"* (Habakkuk 3:16-19). He was declaring that, whatever the natural circumstances are likely to be, he could still negotiate the challenging heights of God's purposes, like a deer on the rugged mountainsides, because the power of God has, in Paul's words, been made perfect in his weakness. Like Paul, he has learned in the Lord's training camp of tough experience that God's grace is sufficient for him, and he is able to do all that God requires him to do through Christ who strengthens him (Philippians 4:13).

To go back to Ephesians 6, the obvious question is: do your boots fit? In other words, is your life founded on the Word of God and on a day-to-day walk with God? Do you regularly turn up for training in God's academy? Do you give as much time to your spiritual health as you do to your physical well-being? How are your spiritual metatarsals?

Or, to put it rather more bluntly, are you getting too big for your boots?

## Are You a Sonoluminescent Saint?

If you were asked, "What is the loudest creature in the ocean?" what would you reply? The huge blue whale, perhaps? Or, those chattering dolphins? Either way, you'd be wrong.

The answer is: a shrimp! Or, to be more correct, trillions of them. According to *The Book of General Ignorance*, the sound of the "shrimp layer" can completely blank out a submarine's sonar system, deafening operators through their headphones. The noise is even louder than the sound of jet taking off and has been compared to the noise of "everyone in the world frying bacon at the same time" – a sizzle with a supersonic bang!

Scientific research has shown that certain species of shrimps have an unusual claw which, when shut rapidly, emits a jet of water travelling at 62mph, producing expanding bubbles of water vapour. Eventually, the bubbles collapse, "creating intense heat (as high as 20,000°C), a loud pop and light".

This is where the word "sonoluminescence" comes in: it describes the phenomenon in which the popping sound produces tiny flashes of light. The shrimps use it to communicate, find mates and stun their enemies. Apparently it is so powerful that it can make dents in ships' propellers! All of which, you may well think, is a parable.

This deep-sea secret is a reminder that an ordered cosmos came into being through a kind of sonoluminescence – though on a vastly different scale – when the sound of God's voice created light (Genesis 1:3); and that, spiritually, the entrance of God's Word continues to give light to minds darkened by sin (Psalm 119:130). It also challenges us as Christians living in the oppressive gloom of a *"crooked and depraved generation"* to *"shine like stars in the universe as we hold forth the word of life"* (Philippians 2:15, 16).

This is sound-generated light, created not merely by the soft glow of a silent example but by the actual proclamation of the Gospel in word as well as deed.

151

It seems unbelievable that a nuclear submarine can be put out of action by a shrimp, but it is worth remembering that the power of the shrimp lies not in its individuality but in its participation with a multitude of others. Solitary shrimps, like loner Christians, make little impact. In one of his Elim Conference Bible studies, Greg Haslam pointed out that if 5 per cent of Britain's population were composed of "Christians of the right kind" (by which I imagine he meant born-again, Bible-believing and obeying, Spirit-filled, wholly committed Christians possessed with a passion to share the Gospel) the country would undergo radical change in every area of its life. The revolving propellers of a secular society would feel the jolt of truth, and through millions of Christians fulfilling their God-given role the sound and light of the Gospel would make a dynamic difference.

In terms of size, most people would probably prefer a lobster to a shrimp, or at least, a king prawn! But size isn't everything. "Alpheous" and "Synalpheous" shrimps have been endowed with a God-given capacity for creating a sound and light show of remarkable power.

In an age when Christians are being encouraged to "think big", it might be a good thing to remember the shrimp. After all, as 1 Corinthians 1:27-29 puts it, *"God chose the foolish things of the world to shame the wise; God chose the weak things [shrimps] of the world to shame the strong [nuclear subs]. He chose the lowly things of this world and the despised things – and the things that are not – to nullify the things that are, so that no one may boast before him."*

Shrimps of the world unite! Renounce your self-centred individualism – you can't "go it alone". Rather, commit yourself to the fellowship of your church, worshipping, praying and working together in Spirit-empowered ministry to a world in need.

Start releasing those God-given bubbles of sound and light in words and deeds that will express your personal commitment to all God desires to do through his church today. Sonoluminescent saints are God's answer to the challenge of our nuclear age.

## Your Most Important Journey Is Just 18 inches Long

In physical terms it's only 18 inches long, but for most people it takes hours, sometimes years, to make the journey, and some never complete it. It's the journey from the head to the heart. Obviously, those 18 inches are only symbolic, since our spiritual anatomy cannot be measured in physical terms, but they are a vivid reminder that the distance between the head and the heart, or, if you prefer, the mind and the will, can be long and difficult.

When Jesus said, *"If you know these things, blessed are you if you do them"* (John 13:17), he recognised the fact that the journey from the head to the heart – the understanding to the will – is not only the longest, but the most important in the world. And sometimes it's the most challenging. But unless we travel that road there is no possibility of experiencing the full purpose of God for our lives.

Many Christians are like people sitting in an airport lounge. They have read all the brochures about their intended destination and, clutching their travel documents, watch other passengers coming and going, but never respond to their own flight call and so never get through the departure gate.

Many Christians never get beyond that departure lounge. They sit there, holding their (biblical) documents, watching the progress of others without venturing further themselves. They can tell you all about the wonderful possibilities such travel opens up, but they never actually make for the gate.

It's all in the mind! They know the facts about the faith and can explain what it all means, but they never really know them experientially. They know about Jesus, but they don't really know him in any deep, personal way. Their faith is intelligent but not interactive with the Spirit and the Word. Their spirituality is coldly cerebral. They can quote Scripture about the joy of the Lord, but they have never experienced *"joy unspeakable and full of glory"* (1 Peter 1:8). They can give teaching on the Holy Spirit without ever knowing what it is to be personally *"strengthened with might by his Spirit in the inner man"*, or to be *"filled with all the fullness of God"* (Ephesians 3:16-18).

This journey certainly does start in the mind. But as Jesus said, *"If you hold to my teaching, you are really my disciples. Then you will know the truth, and the truth will set you free"* (John 8:31, 32). Genuine New Testament spirituality requires the response of the whole personality to its challenging truth, hence Paul's prayer for the Ephesians: *"that the eyes of your heart may be enlightened..."* (Ephesians 1:17-23).

But it is not enough simply to know and understand the great truths of Scripture. The journey never really starts until we get up out of our seats and respond to those truths, believing them, embracing them, taking them to heart, responding to them and obeying them. From this perspective, the Bible is not simply God's word for the church and the world, it is a personal message to me! This is what God wants me to know about himself. This is how he expects me to behave. This is what he desires me to receive. These great New Testament truths set a standard, not only for the church but also for me. I cannot opt out and be pleasing to him.

If, therefore, he says, *"Be holy as I am holy"*, that is what I've got to be. There can be no argument. If he says, *"Seek my face"*, that's what I've got to do – get on my knees and pray. If he says, *"Be filled with the Spirit"*, that is what I have got to seek to be with all my heart. As Mary said, *"Whatever he says to you, do it"* (John 2:5).

For heaven's sake – and earth's – don't just sit there. Get up and go! It's your flight number!

## *Bin the Junk Mail and Invest in the Kingdom*

I've just received another free pen, at least the fifth so far, from a well known bank offering me fantastic interest rates, a very pretty credit card, and stunning buying power – so long as I transfer everything to them. But, like those irritating phone calls from call centres in Hyderabad or Jakarta, who use my name but don't actually know me – and some Christian organisations whose computerised mailshots likewise assure me I'm very much on their electronic hearts and promise to pray for me, and invite me to send them money – they leave me, mild as I am, indignant!

The reality is that, behind the impersonal "intimacy", there is a subtle appeal to my self-interest that will be to their advantage. It's the soft-gloved hand of aggressive marketing that, at its core, is a reflection of the consumerism, material and religious, that characterises the modern age. "Special offer" religion is as dubious as "buy one, get one free" is in the supermarket. It's the "what's in it for me?" syndrome.

In a world fascinated by fashion, infatuated with image, motivated by makeovers and suffering from an obsession with possessions, the words of Jesus in Matthew 6:19-34 have an uncomfortable resonance. He calls those obsessions "paganism" (verses 31 and 32, NIV), and like a divine psychiatrist diagnoses them as symptoms of a major stress factor caused by moral and spiritual schizophrenia (verses 24-31).

Christ's prescription calls for radical treatment: "Get your priorities right" (verse 33) – *"your heavenly Father knows that you need them. But seek first his kingdom and his righteousness, and all these things will be given to you as well."*

Jesus points out that material wealth and possessions are vulnerable to theft and decay (verses 19-21). They are "uncertain riches", and those who structure their lives on them have no real security. But investing in the kingdom of God means taking out shares in an eternal portfolio that will never suffer devaluation or fluctuating interest rates. As Jesus reminds us in this passage, the "small investors" (birds, lilies and grass) are as secure, if not more so, as the "big guys" (Solomon in all his glory).

Investing in the kingdom of God is not a matter of using a calculator to work out your respectable minimum of giving – rounded down to the lower figure – but of recognising God's right to the first place in the total sphere of personal life. It will determine how much we give financially, and how responsibly we give. It will prevent us from spraying money in all directions, answering every emotional appeal that comes through our letterboxes, and making sure that our own church is properly supported in its local and worldwide vision.

Investing in the kingdom means more than spending money, however. It involves lifestyle – seeking the righteousness that comes through faith in Christ and obedience to his Word, embracing the culture of his kingdom and rejecting the values of contemporary society. It means investing time in pursuing the priorities of spiritual life – prayer, reading the Bible, and being involved in the corporate life of the church which provides us with our spiritual home. It means bringing our personal resources, gifts and abilities and making them available to Christ within the fellowship to which, if we are living biblically, we have committed ourselves.

And finally… Jesus said, "The kingdom must come first." Get that priority right and the rest will fall into its rightful place – some of it into the bin.

## *Real Disciples Never Throw Their L Plates Away*

"**A**s if in a dream he found himself, somehow, seated in the driver's seat; as if in a dream he pulled the lever and swung the car round the yard and through the archway… He increased his pace, and as the car devoured the street and leapt forth on the highway through the open country, he was only conscious that he was Toad once more, Toad at his best and highest…" Those who have read *The Wind in the Willows* will remember the story of Mr Toad. After a series of humiliations he is now where he dreamed of being, where indeed he felt he ought to be – in the driver's seat, taking control of things. At last, he has gained his sense of self-worth, and the world would see him as he really was – "Toad at his best and highest".

Alas, it was not to be. For all his self-confidence, Toad crashed. The feel-good factor evaporated in a mess of twisted metal. The truth was that, however ambitious he was, he was not really up to it. Toad is a reminder of an uncomfortable truth: however confident we may feel, however well-trained we are, however experienced we are, however much we may feel fulfilled in our role, however sure we are that we are now in the right place and able to show our true worth, the fact remains that, "just when we're safest, there's a sunset touch" – the day dies. So when Jesus said, *"Without me you can do nothing,"* (John 15:3), he was stating an absolute. We can never afford to discard our L plates, we must always remain learners – "disciples".

Someone has said that the most dangerous time in any driver's experience is immediately after passing the driving test. Gone is the white-knuckled grip on the steering wheel, the strained stare through the windscreen – the freedom of the road beckons, the *Highway Code* is put away. The words, "I've passed!" may be euphoric; they can also be the signal of dangerous self-confidence. In other words, passing tests, fulfilling discipleship courses, attaining diplomas, or even degrees, must never lure us into the illusion that the learning curve has completed its orbit. A disciple is one who never stops learning. But it is not the kind of learning that merely acquires new chunks of information, develops new skills, and achieves personal goals.

The very word "disciple" carries the idea of being more than a mere pupil. It means, "one who not only listens to the words of a teacher, but also seeks to follow the example of the teacher's life." It means more than education, it means emulation; it means more than listening, it means living; it means more than talking the talk, it means walking the walk. Jesus said, *"If you abide in my word, you are truly my disciples, and you will know the truth, and the truth will set you free"* (John 8:31). Similarly in John 15:7-8, he reminds us that only as we live in his word and allow his word to live in us can we produce the kind of fruit that will clearly identify us as real disciples. That simply reinforces his statement in verse 3 – *"Without me you can do nothing."*

The trouble is that, though we easily pay lip-service to those words, in actual practice we tend to ignore them. Our natural abilities, the knowledge and experience we have gained, the access we have to so many brilliant resources, and the confidence that comes from developed skills in life and ministry make us feel less dependent upon consulting him through prayer and his word. But like the experienced fishermen who thought they could safely leave the Carpenter of Nazareth asleep in the back seat of their boat (Mark 4:36f), we need to understand that there is no area of life which we can safely manage without him. We are never self-sufficient.

True disciples understand that. They also understand that real discipleship is more than learning principles, it is a living relationship with a person – Jesus himself. Real disciples don't just learn methods, they love the master and do what he says, (John 14:15-16).

## What's So Wrong With Being "Just a Dad and a Mum"?

Hebrews 11 reads like a list of celebrities: Noah, famous shipbuilder; Abraham, founding father of a great nation; Joseph, distinguished prime minister; Moses, graduate with honours in Egyptology (Acts 7:22) and national leader; Gideon, heroic freedom-fighter; Barak (not Obama!), famous judge; David, warrior and poet king; Samuel, outstanding prophet; and a host of other "big names".

So what, you ask, is Enoch doing in this list? What's so special about him? Certainly he *pleased God"* (verse 5), but there are no great acts of courage and outstanding achievement attributed to him. In fact, all that Genesis 5:21-24 records about him is that he was simply a dad who walked with God! True, Jude 14 mentions that he once prophesied, but otherwise he was "just a dad".

So, why is it that the modern "celebrity culture" causes preachers and writers frequently to say to men, "You're not just a dad, husband or ordinary guy, you are to called to be..." – and there follows some word like "dynamic" or "prophetic", or "God's champion"? And why are Christian women told, "You are not just a housewife, mum, or office-worker, etc., you are called to be a 'princess' or some other 'special' person"? Why are Miriam, the worship-leader, Deborah, the heroic judge, or Esther, the beautiful, courageous woman who saved a nation, the role models, but Jochebed, Moses' devoted mum, and other "just mums" never mentioned? What's wrong with being "just a mum"? Why does everything have to be spiritually "upmarket"?

Of course, as Christians we are called to strive for the highest level of spiritual and personal life (Philippians 3:8-16), but that should not lead us to a superiority complex that makes us look down on ordinary, everyday life as something less significant than being "spiritually enhanced and advanced". *"Do not be proud,"* said Paul, *"but be willing to associate with people of low position. Do not be conceited"* (Romans 12:16).

Severely wounded in the First World War, my father was known simply as a "disabled ex-serviceman". Saved through a Salvation Army open air, he eventually became an active but "ordinary" member of our local Elim church, claiming no special spiritual gift or ministry. Yet the courage with which daily he coped with his disabilities was a powerful example to the family he brought up on the meagre resources of a pension. To me, the youngest of three, he was the miracle-mender of broken toys, the man whose love of music and poetry rubbed off on me, and the friend who took me to watch Hampshire play cricket. He was also, like Enoch, "a man who walked with God". In a way, there was nothing spectacular about him, he was "just a Christian dad", but the young war-time evacuee from London who lived in our home for five years, later becoming a Wing Commander in the RAF, wrote of him, "He was the saintliest man I ever met." Ordinary, but a saint nonetheless.

At a time when we are urged to "discover who you are in God", or to "realise your spiritual potential", or to "fulfil your ministry", etc., it is helpful to remember that Enoch pleased God not by great achievements but simply by believing, in a pagan society, that God existed and was the rewarder of those who diligently sought him (Hebrews 11:5, 6). In that unobtrusive faith he *"walked with God"*, and raised his family.

God is most glorified and pleased when as mums and dads, sons and daughters, carers and nurses, plumbers and secretaries, or whatever, we simply love him for himself, seek him diligently and take our place in his church in humble service. As he says, *"What does the Lord require of you? To act justly and to love mercy and to walk humbly with your God"* (Amos 6:8; see especially 1 Thessalonians 4:11, 12).

# "Crumbs, That Was a Piece of Cake!"

It was a dream of an operation, in more senses than one; but it could just as easily have been a nightmare. There were only 300 of them facing an army of thousands of highly armed and battle – hardened troops. With their bizarre "equipment" they remind you of World War II Dad's Army being mobilized to fight the threat of invading German Panzer divisions with little more than pitchforks and other assorted implements.

Their commanding officer didn't look much of a prospect, either. He certainly hadn't graduated from a military academy. Psychiatrists would have pointed to his low self – esteem; Sir Alan Sugar of *The Apprentice* programme would have cut his interview short in five minutes, contemptuously barking, "You're fired!" and black-clad Anne Robinson would have fixed him with a deprecating smile and said, dismissively, "You *are* the weakest link, goodbye". Most denominational selection boards would have shaken wise heads and said, "Nice young man, but definitely not leadership material."

Oddly enough, God didn't agree with the experts. But then, he often doesn't! He actually chose Gideon – see Judges 6:11f and follow the story through the next chapters – precisely because here was a man who knew his own limitations and would have to rely totally upon divine enabling.

That's the reason God chooses most of his best people – see 1 Corinthians 1:26–29 and 2 Corinthians 1:8–10; 12:7–10. Put in other words, *"He cares for the humble, but keeps his distance from the proud"* (Psalm 138:6 NLT).

Unlike many so-called leaders, God was wonderfully patient with his hesitant hero, giving him the opportunity to "ask a friend" to accompany him on a secret mission into the enemy camp. Breathlessly listening outside one of the tents, Gideon hears the gruff voices discussing a dream and its meaning: a cake of barley bread rolls down the hill and flattens a soldier's tent. It's ludicrous — Weetabix wins! But what he hears moves him to worship, quickens his faith, and inspires him to action (Judges 7:10-18).

Trumpets in the night, the crash of broken pottery, three hundred shouting Hebrews, and three hundred flaming torches are enough – enough, that is, when God is on your side – to rout an army! Outnumbered they may be, and completely "out-gunned" in terms of weaponry, this Israelite "Dad's Army" conquers the might of Midian.

From one point of view, it was, as we sometimes say, "a piece of cake"; but actually it was no easy victory. It called for faith in the promises of God, courage to take risks in obedience to His Word, and determination to see things through to the end. There is no greater tribute to Gideon and his "gallant three hundred" than in Judges 8:4 which shows them reaching the river Jordan, "exhausted, yet keeping up the pursuit".

That's the way it is. Spiritual victories are not won by superior human strength but by obedient faith – faith which nonetheless is prepared to go the whole way with God.

The exhausted Son of God in Gethsemane, the apostle of 2 Corinthians 4:8–12 who, Gideon-like, holds the torch of the Gospel in a "jar of clay", and a host of other men and women who have been willing to "wholly follow the Lord" whatever the cost – are the real heroes of the Faith.

Actually, there is more to this tent-demolishing "piece of cake" than you realise. Its secret ingredients are faith, obedience, courage and persistence, specially blended with the oil of the Spirit to give it a flavour and texture that is truly unique. In fact, I'm tempted to call it rock cake! But whatever name we give it, it is, as "Mr Kipling" in the adverts would say, "Exceedingly good!"

# Keep Watching "The Apprentice" – The Person, not the Programme!

Grey, grizzled and grumpy, Sir Alan Sugar casts a baleful eye over the ambitious young hopefuls who aspire to join his company, then one by one he tears apart their pretentious claims to business acumen and with a pointing finger at some wilting would-be entrepreneur growls, "You're fired."

*The Apprentice,* watched by millions of fascinated viewers, presents the harsh face of the ruthless competitiveness of the modern world, where the lives of multitudes of young men and women – and sometimes their families – are sacrificed on the altars of professional and commercial success.

It was, I think, the biblical scholar C H Dodd who, in a completely different context, coined the term "apprenticeship" to describe the meaning of Jesus' words in John's Gospel: *"... the Son can do nothing by himself; he can do only what he sees his Father doing, because whatever the Father does the Son also does..."* (5:19-20). Dodd suggested that what the boy Jesus had been in his earthly father's carpenter's shop in Nazareth, watching a master craftsman at his work and serving an apprenticeship in shaping wood, the man Jesus became in the cosmic workshop of his heavenly Father; still watching and working in partnership, but now shaping the lives of damaged human beings and a broken world into "something beautiful, something good". It's a pleasing thought, not least because we too, as Christ's disciples, are called to be apprentices in the same "firm". Jesus said, *"Take my yoke upon you and learn from me..."* (Matthew 11:29) – accept an apprenticeship with me and come and "learn the trade"!

But what a different kind of apprenticeship! In contrast to the aggressive competitiveness of the modern world, Jesus calls us to work with him as he worked with his father. The workshop may be global, but this is no soulless multi-national corporation engaged in ruthless exploitation of resources and people for the sake of sheer profit, but a "family business" in which *"the Father loves the Son and shows him all he does",* so that the Son can reproduce the Father's custom-built designs and quality workmanship. As I know from my apprenticeship days, watching a master craftsman at work will teach you more than all the "how to do it" books in the world. The Master is far better than the manual. But you do have to watch him.

In contrast to Sir Alan Sugar's unsweetened man-management (surely, only for the cameras?), Jesus actually calls failing people into partnership: *"Come to me, all you who are weary and burdened, and I will give you rest."* Instead of rasping "You're fired!" at people who are "not fit for purpose", Jesus offers grace to the hopeless: *"A bruised reed he will not break, and a smouldering wick he will not snuff out"* (Matthew 12:20). He doesn't discard people who have failed to make the grade, but calls them into a transforming relationship with himself.

Jesus is not a "control-freak" or an office bully. He is *"gentle and humble".* God loves him and points to him as a perfect example of spiritual leadership, delighted at his refusal, unlike some of his followers who claim such leadership, to posture in ostentatious public displays of self-importance (Matthew 12:15-19). Here is "The Apprentice" who wins the Father's approval and receives the ultimate prize (Philippians 2:8-11). And here is the divine role-model on whom our own apprenticeship and leadership must be moulded. We must allow him to take the reins; we must *"take his yoke"* and *"learn from"* his example and teaching. In so doing, we will discover the secret of a liberated life. In the words of Matthew 12:20, *"Walk with me and work with me – watch how I do it. Learn the unforced rhythms of grace. I won't lay anything heavy or ill-fitting on you. Keep company with me and you'll learn how to live freely and lightly"* (The Message).

## *"Hmm, Blue Screen!"*

"**H**mm, blue screen!" my cheerful neighbour exclaimed as he contemplated my computer. Andy works in IT with a large company and it was to him I fled when the screen went blank just as I was completing an article for *Direction.* "I'm in dead trouble," I called through the intercom of his flat and was more than relieved when his voice crackled in reply, "Hang on, I'll be with you in a minute." I had pressed every key in a vain attempt to recall the lost work and was overcome by a feeling of helpless frustration. My only hope was with an expert who would be willing to come to my assistance. "Blue screen", to a computer-illiterate like me sounded fatal, perhaps some dreaded electronic form of mad cow disease. Even Andy had some difficulty in dealing with it, but to my huge relief, the screen flickered back into life and the (to me) precious article reappeared. Andy was more than a friendly neighbour, he was a hero! He had retrieved something I had feared was lost forever.

This incident came back to mind while reading Paul's words in Colossians 2: 13-15, *"When you were dead in your sins and in the uncircumcision of your sinful nature, God made you alive with Christ..."* The truth is that all of us have "lost it" spiritually and morally. The screen has gone blank because, *"there is no-one righteous, not even one, there is no-one who understands, no-one who seeks God...for all have sinned and fallen short of the glory of God"* (Romans 3:10-11, 23). We are faced with a moral "blue screen" and nothing we can do will restore our lost innocence.

My only hope was to face facts and admit that I had "lost it" and then seek expert help. That admission of failure did nothing for my ego, but it was the first step to recovery. One of the most difficult things for human beings to do is to admit failure. While discredited politicians and failed celebrities are quick to plead "I've done nothing wrong" and slow to say, "I'm sorry," the rest of us are just as quick to point accusing fingers at them while repeating the same self-excusing mantras. But the truth is that, as far as personal righteousness is concerned, all our screens are blank. We have lost it, and the sooner we face up to the facts and seek help, the better it will be. We can go on tapping away at the keys of self-righteousness and self-justification and find some kind of satisfaction in the fact that we are trying to do our best, but the fact remains that it is all to no purpose. We can never recover our lost innocence by our own efforts, however sincere we may be. In Paul's words, we are *"dead in our sins - without hope and without God in the world"* (Ephesians 2: 12).

But that is where the "expert" comes in. *"You see just at the right time, when we were still powerless, Christ died for the ungodly"* and *"God demonstrates his own love for us in this: While we were still sinners, Christ died for us"* (Romans 5:6-7). Like my "hero" Andy, God knows how to restore what has otherwise been irretrievably lost. As Paul points out to the Colossians, because on the cross Jesus paid the debt we owed God and suffered the penalty that debt incurred, God is able to *"forgive our trespasses",* our law-breaking, not just our "mistakes", and then totally wipe out the record that stood against us. He deals with the virus of sin that has caused our moral monitors to crash and is able *"to cleanse us from all unrighteousness"* (1 John 1:8-10) and restore us to a new relationship with himself (Romans 5:1-2). But only those who are humble and honest enough to admit they've blown it and are willing to seek the "expert's" help have any hope of that restoration. Thank God, he's always on call – *"Call upon me in the day of trouble; I will deliver you"* (Psalm 50:14-15). Otherwise, we're left hopelessly staring at a "blue screen"!

# Don't Lose Your "Cutting Edge" When You Build For God

The rhythm of swinging the axe brought a certain feeling of pleasure, especially when he felt the blade bite into the tree. Out in the open in a riverside wood, this young student was enjoying himself, not only in the physical activity, but because he was contributing to an inspiring venture – the building of a new college for the "school of ministry" to which he belonged. The demand for a new building reflected the growing success of the school, and he was proud to be part of it. Then, suddenly – disaster! The axe-head left the shaft and following a trajectory of its own fell with an undistinguished plop into the river. To add to his chagrin, it wasn't even his! "*Alas,*" he cried to the Principal, "*it was borrowed!*"

This delightful cameo from 2 Kings 6:1-7 gives us an insight into the training of prophets in Elijah's day as well as showing how his own prophetic ministry was validated by signs and wonders during an age of national apostasy. It reminds us that in the excitement of building something for God it is possible to lose your "cutting edge"!

Why the axe-head left the handle is not explained, but anyone who has chopped wood or used a hammer knows that, if you do not keep a careful check, things do "fly off the handle" (this applies to people as well as tools!). However, at least this man was humble and honest. Unlike Samson (Judges 16:20), he made no attempt to cover up his loss by going through the normal routine with an empty handle; he knew where he had "lost it" and sought for prophetic intervention. Only that supernatural involvement restored what he had lost.

For us, the "cutting edge" is the Spirit-anointed application of the Word of God to our inner spiritual life (Hebrews 4:12) and to our engagement with the powers of darkness in terms both of spiritual warfare (Ephesians 6:17-18) and the proclamation of the Gospel (2 Corinthians 10:3-6). Lose that, and however impressive the structures

167

we erect may be, whether in terms of splendid new buildings or in the latest methods of "doing church", we cannot fulfil the purpose for which God has called us. This is true, not only for movements or churches; it applies to individual lives as well.

Corporately or personally, we cannot, to quote William Blake, "build Jerusalem" if our "sword sleeps in our hand". *"It is not by might not by power, but by my Spirit says the Lord"* (Zechariah 4:6).

The challenges facing the church today demand that we carefully examine the state of the theological and practical tools we are using. Whatever other skills a Bible college may seek to develop in its students, unless it teaches them to base their thinking and practice on the Word of God, it has failed in its duty to them, the church and the outside world. Unless they emerge from its classrooms with a strong biblical theology and are able to apply that to their personal lifestyle and impart it through their ministry under the direction and dynamic of the Holy Spirit it has lost its "cutting edge". The same is true for every movement, every local church and every individual Christian life. Unless we constantly examine out spiritual technology, however "state of the art" we think it is, and ensure that at all times it is firmly connected to the final authority of Scripture and "what the Spirit is saying to the churches" we are in danger of "losing it". As this student discovered, only the prophetic word and supernatural intervention restored to him what he had lost.

Only through the Word and the Spirit can we fulfil our mission. There is no alternative for any of us whether as churches or as individuals. Of that essential "cutting edge" we have to say, like David when he called for the sword with which he slew Goliath (1 Samuel 21:9), *"There is none like that, give it to me."*

# *And Finally*

# *Reflections*

## Hearing Voices in the Valley

When Tennyson's "noble six hundred" charged into the valley of death it was amidst the roar of cannon, the thunder of hooves, the clash of steel, the neighing of horses and the shouts and screams of fighting and dying men.

When the lonely prophet Ezekiel made his way down into the valley of dry bones it was amidst the brooding silence of a place where a vast army of scattered bones lay, whitened and dried, under the forbidding glare of a relentless sun.

*The Charge of the Light Brigade* told the story of a heroic, but misdirected, battle in the Crimean war; Ezekiel's vision (37:1-14) painted a picture of the defeat, disintegration and despair – but also the only hope – of a nation carried away into captivity.

Just recently, in the course of preparing a message on another subject, I briefly revisited Ezekiel's valley of dry bones, and whilst there I was reminded of the contrast between Tennyson's clamorous epic of tragedy and triumph and the eerie stillness of Ezekiel's vision of a nation's decline and fall. Yet, pausing there, I caught the sound of voices in the valley of death.

*"Son of man, can these bones live?"* (v 3). God's voice is challenging Ezekiel's prophetic integrity. After all, prophets are supposed always to have something to say, so, "Come on, Ezekiel, you're a prophet, give us a word from the Lord!"

*"O Sovereign Lord, you alone know."* Ezekiel's low-toned whisper confesses his utter dependence upon God. Some men would have called together a committee to discuss God's question; some would have talked vaguely about "reconstruction", some about classifying the bones and placing them in a museum where their historic significance could be studied; some would have suggested clearing the site and burying the past; and some would have organised a

"celebration event" – because you've got to "make a positive statement" even if you're not quite sure what it should be!

But Ezekiel quietly says, "I don't know what to say, Lord, the ball is in your court." And God answers him, as he always does when men humbly seek his face. God's answer to the situation in the valley of death is twofold. First, proclaim the Word: *"Prophesy to these bones and say to them, 'Dry bones, hear the word of the Lord'"* (v 4). Second, call for the Spirit: *"Prophesy to the breath..."* (vv 9, 10; and note v 14). The Word and the Spirit – these are the agents of spiritual renewal, whether it be of a spiritually bankrupt nation, a "dead" church, a dried-out ministry or a desert-like personal experience.

It was the Word and the Spirit that brought cosmos out of chaos at the creation (Genesis 1:1-3), and it is that dynamic combination of revelation and regeneration that creates and sustains every dimension of life. There are no viable alternatives.

Unless the Church believes, proclaims and obeys the Word of God she has no real credibility or authority; but that belief, proclamation and lifestyle must be based on *"the whole counsel of God"* (Acts 20:27) – on his revelation of himself, his grace and his sovereign will *"in all the scriptures"* (Luke 24:27), not just in the bits we prefer! And such preaching, teaching and living must be accompanied by complete dependence on the Holy Spirit. No authentic Christian life and ministry can take place without his enabling. *"It is not by might, nor by power, but by my Spirit, says the Lord of Hosts."*

Ezekiel's valley was a place where the dynamic impact of the Word and the sweeping winds of the Spirit alone brought transformation. Charismatic cavalry charges are undeniably exciting, but it is the Word and the Spirit that transform the valley of death. We need to remember that God confirms his Word – not our methods – by signs and wonders. Perhaps we should talk less and listen more!

# The Secret of the Real "Da Vinci code"!

It has fired the imagination of millions, inspired books, TV programmes, newspaper articles and a costly lawsuit. *The Da Vinci Code* – a mishmash of highly speculative theories about the so-called descendants of Jesus and the whereabouts of the cup used at the Last Supper – has no historical or theological credibility; yet it has claimed enormous popularity. That itself is the evidence of the yearning modern people have for something beyond the cold, grey meaninglessness of our materialistic, secular age.

There is, in fact, a much more authentic "Da Vinci code" found in the writings of Leonardo da Vinci himself. Referring to his invention of a submarine, he wrote in his Notebooks that he had decided not to disclose the plans, "on account of the evil nature of men". They would use the invention, he said, "to practise assassinations in the bottom of the seas". Too true!

The real Da Vinci code was in fact a "code of practice" that took into account the fallenness of human nature and asked serious questions about the moral implications of an otherwise exciting scientific advance.

In his book *The Seventh Enemy*, Ronald Higgins has drawn the striking contrast between Leonardo's code and that of the physicist Enrico Fermi, who in 1945 was working on the first atomic tests in America. Questioned about the morality of his work, Fermi snapped, "Don't bother me with your conscientious scruples. After all, the thing's superb physics." Higgins comments, "For all the rigour, dedication and courage involved in research, there is a tragic naivety in the notion that it can be pursued or applied in a kind of moral vacuum... For knowledge brings power and men abuse power..."

Alfred Nobel, the inventor of dynamite, recognised the moral implications of all human actions when, appalled by the vast destructive use to which men put his discoveries, he spent most of his fortune in instituting the famous Peace Prize that bears his name. He wanted to mitigate at least something of the horrors dynamite had placed in the hands of men.

The ethical tensions that increasing scientific knowledge and its technological advances bring are a major dilemma for us today. How far should industrial nations go in the pursuit of the prestigious but extravagantly costly exploration of space? How far should medical science go in genetic advance? What are the moral boundaries in research involving stem cells and "designer babies"? What are the political and economic limits for the ambitious exploitation of the Earth's resources and the pollution of its environment by the rich nations, when millions starve in horrific squalor? Is there no code of conduct for humankind? The questions are endless, but they need to be asked – and answered.

Why do people get so absorbed in dubious fiction when the big questions demand an answer? Why does the Christian Church get so absorbed in tinkering with its ecclesiastical infrastructures and its introspective self-awareness when there's a world out there that needs a straightforward, Spirit-empowered proclamation of the Gospel of Christ and his saving power? How will she answer at the judgement seat?

Why do Christians spend so much time on their personal happiness, material well-being and spiritual self-indulgence? When our pursuit of spiritual freedom makes us indifferent to the heartbreak of a broken world and we fail to understand the effect our personal lifestyle has on those around us, we break the code of conduct enshrined in the words of 1 Corinthians 8:9-13 and James 2:12. Make sure you read them. Smiling "super saints" and "successful" churches need a Da Vinci code as much as science does.

## *Understanding the Times*

**J** B Phillips, whose *New Testament in Modern English* was the splendid forerunner of the many new versions of the Scriptures now filling our bookshops, tells of his experience in handling the original Greek text. He says that he felt like an electrician working in an old house in which it was not possible to turn off the mains supply. The very words were "live", and every now and then he received a "shock".

One cannot read the New Testament without sensing the electric surge of expectancy and urgency crackling through its pages when the current of its message arcs across the electrodes of present experience and future hope.

Hear Jesus' cry: *"We must carry on the work of him that sent me while the daylight lasts. Night is coming…"* (John 9:4, J B Phillips).

And James: *"The Lord's coming is near… the Judge is standing at the door!"* (James 5:8 and 9).

Listen to Peter: *"The end of all things is at hand"* (1 Peter 4:7).

Hear John: *"Dear children, this is the last hour…"* (1 John 2:18).

And finally, Paul: *"The present time is of the highest importance – it is time to wake up to reality. Every day brings God's salvation nearer. The night is nearly over, the day has almost dawned…"* (Romans 13:11-14, J B Phillips).

Paul's words about *"understanding the present time"* (verse 11, NIV), are set in the most down-to-earth passage in his letter. They are not about prophetic time-charts or identifying a contemporary "man of sin"; they're about realising the urgency of living for Christ in a doomed world. They're about personal holiness in terms of good citizenship (verses 1 to 5), about paying the right amount of income tax (verses 6 and 7), about living debt-free (verse 8), about loving one's neighbour (verses 9 and 10). Think of filling in your tax forms while remembering that Jesus is coming soon!

Paul's readers lived in a society dominated by the lust for power, pleasure and personal gain. Rome was a city where pagan temples thrust their architectural arrogance above the skyline (like the temples of commerce today); where the rich lounged in self-indulgent luxury and the poor were huddled together in stinking slums; where obscene laughter echoed from its taverns, and prostitutes paraded its streets; where idle crowds filled its arenas and greedy businessmen bargained in its markets. The picture is all too familiar!

Against that background, Paul calls for uncompromising personal holiness (verses 12 and 13) and sounds an urgent trumpet call for spiritual warfare: *"Let us arm ourselves for the fight of the day"* (v12, J B Phillips).

There's a war on! The aggressive thrust of materialism and humanism must be challenged by a Church wielding weapons that are *"mighty in pulling down strongholds"* (2 Corinthians 10:4, 5 and see Ephesians 5:10f).

Moreover, Paul urges us to embrace a dynamic relationship with Jesus: *"Let us be Christ's men from head to foot, and give no chance to the flesh to have its fling,"* is Phillips's imaginative rendering of verse 14.

*"Understanding the times"* is not about fanciful speculation about computers in Brussels, or the significance of ID cards, or the shifting patterns of the kaleidoscope of contemporary politics; it is about recognising that our final salvation is getting closer, that the purposes of God are moving inexorably towards their climax, that the "night" (the reign of the powers of darkness) is nearly over – dawn is breaking over the horizons of a lost world.

It means realising that we need to rouse ourselves from self-indulgent complacency, get up and start living for God, refusing to compromise, and engaging in Spirit-empowered evangelism. Above all, it means seeking a daily "close encounter" with Jesus.

## *How to Live in the Last Days*

For many years, the cartoon figure of an elderly man in a flat cap and shabby overcoat holding aloft a banner bearing the words 'The end is nigh!' has been a figure of fun for most people because they think that such warnings need not be taken too seriously. Even the threat of rogue states developing weapons of mass destruction, warnings of ecological disaster through global warming, the rise of world-threatening terrorism and the possibility of economic meltdown, have not removed the complacency of modern society about the likelihood of a coming day of judgement – a mindset shared by many who claim to be Christians.

The New Testament knows of no such complacency; its pages vibrate with an urgent anticipation of the end of the age. Jesus himself (John 9:4), Paul (Romans 13:11-14), James (5:7-8) and John (1 John 2:18), spoke and lived like men conscious of living on the border between time and eternity. In the same way, Peter declares, *"The end of all things is at hand"* (1 Peter 4:7).

Peter's words about *"the end of all things"* may be taken in two ways. He may be saying that nothing is permanent – that all "things", however substantial they seem to be, have a limited shelf-life. As Shakespeare put it in *The Tempest*,

> *The cloud-clapp'd towers, the gorgeous palaces,*
> *The solemn temples, the great globe itself,*
> *Yes, all which it inherit shall dissolve,*
> *And like this insubstantial pageant faded,*
> *Leave not a rack behind.*

If that is so, our obsession with "things" – possessions, money, status and the rest – is folly. As it is, our much-prized BMWs are in danger of becoming BBTs – ultimately being towed to the crusher's yard and ignominiously recycled as baked bean tins! Nothing lasts. Moreover, as Peter writes in his second letter, *"the day of the Lord will come like a thief, and then the heavens will pass away with a roar and the heavenly bodies will be burned up and dissolved and the earth and the works that are done on it will be exposed"* (2 Peter 3:10f). As Jesus pointed out in Matthew 6:19-34, only investment in the kingdom of heaven is fire-proof and decay-proof. To think otherwise is a form of paganism (Matthew 6:32 NIV).

The second way of understanding *"the end of all things"* is to see it in terms of completion. "This is the way the world ends," sighed T.S. Eliot, "not with a bang but a whimper." But he was wrong. The Bible foretells not whimpers, but angelic shouts, celestial trumpets, the all-powerful voice of the Lord and the massed choirs of the redeemed. The paradoxes of history will be resolved as God's eternal purpose of heading everything up under Christ is realised (Ephesians 1:9-10), the distortions of a creation under judgement will be smoothed into incredible beauty (Romans 8:19-23), and men and women whose lives have been "ruined by the fall" will be transformed into the glory of likeness to Christ (1 Corinthians 15:51f; Philippians 3:20-21). The very fires that melt the planets are but the cosmic bulldozers clearing the ruins in order for a new creation to rise (2 Peter 3:10-13). The *"end of all things"* is not caused by an accidental match dropped into a box of global fireworks; it is rather a "controlled explosion" which makes the universe safe for a magnificent new development (Hebrews 12:26-29).

As Peter points out in 1 Peter 4:7f, living on the frontiers of the apocalypse demands an appropriate lifestyle. It calls for a sound, disciplined mind, a watchful, praying spirit, a loving heart totally committed to the welfare of the local fellowship of believers and the willingness to use personal gifts and abilities in the service of God by his empowerment and for his glory. These are absolute essentials. *"What kind of people ought you to be?"* he asks in 2 Peter 3:11-12. And his reply is, *"You ought to live holy and godly lives as you look forward to the day of God and speed its coming".* That's the only way to live in the last days.

## *Following in the Footsteps of God's Freedom Fighter*

It was one of those brief encounters that happen in a matter of minutes, but leave a lifetime's legacy.

Many years ago while fulfilling a preaching engagement in the city of Hull, I took time out to visit the house in which William Wilberforce, God's "freedom fighter" against the evil slave trade that shamed Britain in the 18th and 19th centuries, spent much of his life. In one of the rooms there was a picture that showed the shocking way in which slaves were transported from Africa to the Americas. I stood for a long time trying to imagine the misery of those slaves lying chained side by side amidst appalling conditions in creaking ships battered by Atlantic gales. Suddenly, I heard a sound and turned to see the only other person in the room: he was black! It was then the awful truth came home: this is what my people did to his people.

The encounter was brief but painful. The only mitigation lay in the fact that it was a white man, William Wilberforce, who led the fight against the evil of the slave trade. It was not, of course, an entirely "black and white" issue – there were not a few greedy Africans who sold their compatriots into slavery – but the fact remains that it took 20 years and ten defeats in Parliament before Wilberforce's bill was finally passed and given Royal Assent 200 years ago on 25th March 1807.

Powerful merchants, compromising politicians and complacent religious leaders resisted the call for abolition (even Lord Nelson fired a verbal broadside from HMS Victory against what he called "the damnable doctrine of Wilberforce"), and it took another 20 years before the fight was finally over.

It is easy, with hindsight, to assume that I (and you) would have been on Wilberforce's side; but how sure can I be that I would not have followed popular opinion? After all, in most people's view Wilberforce was a wealthy evangelical Anglican "do-gooder", forever going on about something that was of no real concern to ordinary people. Moreover, most of the bishops opposed him, and if a "celebrity" like Nelson was against him why should I support him? In fact, how sure am I that I would not have just ignored it all and minded my own business?

Perhaps the answers to these questions lie in my (and your) attitude to the moral and social enslavements of modern society. How concerned am I – really concerned – about the fact that a third of all the money pouring into the pockets of criminals comes from "people trafficking", the modern-day slave trade that lures thousands into the sex industry? Am I really deeply moved by the fact that millions of my fellow human beings are enslaved by political tyranny, poverty, religious persecution, drug addiction, gambling, all-consuming materialism, alcohol abuse, pornography, and soul – and body – destroying sexual promiscuity – to name only a few of the harsh facts of the 21st-century world?

Does my concern drive me to my knees in fervent intercessory prayer? Does it move me to get involved in my church's outreach to the lost? Do I support the agencies that are ministering into areas of social and political concern? Do I write to my MP on issues that affect the well-being of my country? Do I ever raise my voice on anything? Or am I so concerned with being "spiritual" and seeking personal prosperity that I don't bother with newspapers and all that stuff and am blissfully unaware of the cries of the slaves of sin? If so, I need to turn to Luke 4:17-19 and 2 Corinthians 5:16-21.

In the quietness of Wilberforce's home and in that brief encounter with the other man I felt deeply ashamed and moved by what my people had done to his; yet mingled with the sadness was deep gratitude for the godly Christian white man who fought against all odds for the freedom of the slaves. Here was the faith that had overcome the world, and here was a faith that still challenges me about my personal response to the needs of a world enslaved by the powers of darkness.

Am I, like Jesus, "moved with compassion" as I see the multitudes? Am I willing to be a freedom fighter for the truth of God's word and the liberation of broken men and women? Or do I just look the other way? Because, after all, setting captives free lies at the heart of the Gospel.

## Don't Demolish "Jerusalem"!

It was written in 1804 by William Blake as the preface to a poem celebrating the genius of the poet John Milton and first sung at meetings celebrating the fight for women's suffrage. The magic of Sir Hubert Parry's rousing tune caught the imagination of the public, making it a favourite at a wide spectrum of events from Women's Institute meetings to national celebrations, great sporting occasions and the flag-waving enthusiasm of the Last Night of the Proms.

Recently, however, it has come under attack. The Dean of Southwark Cathedral has banned it because it is not in the glory of God. He has a point, of course, because it contains no direct reference to God; as Sally Magnusson in her book *Glorious Things* observes, it is "a hymn to human aspiration rather than divine inspiration". It is certainly not God-centred, but in that it joins not a few vague modern worship songs which would make visitors to our churches wonder about exactly to whom, or about whom, we are actually singing.

It has also been accused of being nationalistic; but genuine love of country is not necessarily jingoistic – many of the Psalms reveal a passionate love for Jerusalem, and Paul's heartfelt cry for his nation's salvation (Romans 10:1) reveals a Spirit-inspired patriotism.

William Blake was a complex man, part mystic, part visionary, with much of his poetry difficult to decipher. In *Jerusalem* he seems to refer to the legend that Christ once visited Glastonbury with Joseph of Arimathea, but his response is actually a series of questions – "And *did* those feet...?" The last line of the verse, with its reference to "those dark satanic mills", gives us a clue as to what was really in his mind.

Strangely enough, that line caused the clergy in St Margaret's Westminster to ban the hymn because "it discriminated against people living in the city"! That seems about as daft as the effect the words had on my youthful mind. To me, one of the "dark satanic mills" was a sinister-looking, black, sail-less old windmill standing alongside a country road, which gave me the creeps every time I passed it on my bike.

It seems almost certain that Blake had in mind those infamous cotton mills where, in the days of the Industrial Revolution, little children were forced to work until they dropped, and the factories where the age of the machine had turned their parents into factory slaves. Blake joined his voice to the growing outcry of protest, much of it coming from the Evangelical leaders of the day like Wilberforce and Shaftesbury.

In fact, you can't really understand the poem until you realise that, in its original form, it ended with a quotation from Numbers: *"Would to God that all the Lord's people were Prophets"* (11:29). That gives it a new meaning. It is a cry for prophetic intervention.

Exactly what Blake's *Jerusalem* stood for is not clear, though it was probably shaped by the vision of the holy city in Revelation 21 – a society peaceful and secure under God's righteous reign. To this end he rides his Elijah-like "chariot of fire" and calls for his "bow of gold" and "arrows of desire", and, unsleeping sword in hand, commits himself to an uncompromising "mental fight" for righteousness. Maybe he thought only in political terms, but his weapons were "weapons of mass construction" forged by a passion to fight for a better society by challenging the evils of his day.

*Jerusalem* may not appeal to our theological or musical taste, but before we demolish it as mere sentimental patriotism we should listen to its call for a prophetic response to the challenge of our day. We, too, need to reach for the *"weapons of our warfare which are mighty through God to pull down strongholds"* (2 Corinthians 10:3-5). As never before, our world needs the people of God to fight on all fronts against the spiritual, moral and social wrongs that enslave the human race.

## Living in Harmony with Heaven

It was a moment of utter horror. As the pianist for one of the great Elim Easter Monday rallies in the Royal Albert Hall, I struck the note for the opening song – and immediately realised it was two octaves too high! With hunched shoulders I waited for the inevitable... and it happened. Several thousand voices climbed impossible heights, then disintegrated and fell to earth like – a shower of sparks from a failed rocket. The memory still causes an embarrassed shudder.

Finding the right note is not simply a musical maxim however, it is the key to everything.

Lloyd C Douglas, the author of *The Robe*, the best-seller that became a famous film, tells how, in his student days, he rented an apartment next door to an elderly music teacher. Every morning they went through the same routine: Douglas would knock on his neighbour's door and ask, "Well, what's the good news?" The music teacher would take his tuning fork, strike it on his invalid chair and intone, "That's Middle C. It was Middle C yesterday; it will be Middle C tomorrow, and in a thousand years from now it will still be Middle C. The tenor upstairs sings flat; the piano across the hall is out of tune, but that, my friend, is still Middle C!"

In the midst of a world of changing values and clashing discords, the old man had found one constant factor on which he knew he could rely – Middle C.

For the Christian, Jesus Christ is that one certain reality. As Hebrews 13:8 says, he is *"the same yesterday and today and forever"*. He is the one unchanging centre around which the universe revolves. Scientists may speculate endlessly about the origins and possible end of the cosmos, but the New Testament declares that "yesterday" the Lord was the Creator of all things (John 1:1-3), and "today" in him everything holds together (Colossians 1:15-17; Hebrews 1:3). And "tomorrow" this same Jesus will come in a final act of absolute authority to wind up history (1 Corinthians 15:23-27; Hebrews 1:10-12).

Jesus is the "Middle C" of our personal lives. His love never wanes, his wisdom is never overtaken by the march of science, his power never diminishes through wear and tear, his teaching never passes its sell-by date, and his grace is always sufficient for us. He never suffers from changing moods, never loses concentration – he *"neither slumbers of sleeps"* – and he is always refreshingly and dynamically the same.

Like the old music teacher, we too live in a world of bewildering and ever accelerating change. Values change, the structures of society change, fashions change, the map of the world changes, our friends change, and we change. "It's a different world," we say... and often we don't like what we see and hear.

Like "the tenor upstairs and the piano across the hall", the world is "flat" and out of tune – because men and women have rebelled against their Creator God and tried to write their own score without using Middle C. But you can't! Jesus Christ is the basic note on which the whole symphony of life depends. Without him, there is no meaning, and no true harmony in life – because without him there can be no peace with God.

His teaching, his life, his death on the cross, and his triumphant resurrection are the only hope for our troubled world and our personal lives. That is why he is "Middle C". Only through him can we be restored to fellowship with God. Only through his teaching can we learn the truth that will give us the "unforced rhythms of grace" and inner peace, and only through his power can we find the strength to be the kind of people we ought to be. As he said, *"Apart from me you can do nothing"* (John 15:5).

## Read Jude's "Email"!

He had intended it to be a long, leisurely, warm and friendly letter in which he would share his thoughts about their mutual faith. Instead it became an urgent "email" dealing with a spiritual crisis in the church to which he was writing. Jude, probably one of the natural brothers of Jesus, explains his reasons in the opening verses of the short epistle which bears his name.

This church had been invaded by a group of so-called teachers who were spiritually suspect. In his commentary on Jude, Michael Green points out that, "Physically they became immoral. Intellectually, they became arrogant. Spiritually, they became disobedient to the Lord." He continues, "Progressive morality and 'progressive thinking' often go hand in hand with progressive deafness to the voice of God". History repeats itself – the situation which aroused Jude's concern is still with us. *"The faith once delivered to the saints"* is still challenged by those who desire to modernise its doctrines and modify its ethical requirements in keeping with "contemporary trends" of thought and practice.

Jude's response is uncompromising. Alongside a devastating exposé of the emptiness of the false teachers – they are *"clouds without rain"*, full of fault-finding and self-promotion – he reveals their divisiveness and the lack of the Holy Spirit's annointing (verses 12-16), and then calls upon the members of the church to respond to the challenge by *"building yourselves up in your most holy faith and praying in the Holy Spirit, keep yourselves in the love of God, waiting for the mercy of our Lord Jesus Christ that leads to eternal life"* (20-21 ESV). It is a message the modern church needs to heed. There are voices, some of them Evangelical, calling for subtle adjustments to the historic faith in order to meet the challenge of so-called "new insights" on doctrinal issues and moral and ethical standards. The church's new clothes must be cut to meet the demands of the latest fashions, otherwise she will be regarded as outdated and thereby unattractive to the world she seeks to win.

In contrast, Jude calls for a re-affirmation of the historic faith. He calls it *"your most holy faith,"* because it was *"delivered to the people of God"* as an inheritance which must never be compromised. It is the *"word of his grace which is able to build you up and give you an inheritance"* (Acts 20:32) it is the living and life-giving word which alone can create and sustain spiritual faith and a God-honouring lifestyle. Jude's call is for an uncompromising return to biblical truth and biblical standards of practice and personal behaviour. He is saying, "Whatever the latest trends in theology and cultural standards may be, get back to the Word of God: read it, pray over it, ask the Holy Spirit to help you understand it, take time to ponder its meaning, build on its truths, let them challenge you, inspire you to worship, and move you to respond in faith and obedience. Then you will pray effectively, keep within the orbit of God's love, and have a forward looking hope."

By the way, this "email" is not addressed to leaders of the church, but to individual members – *"But you...building yourselves up..."* The trouble is, only a minority of us ever download it! That's why the church is so out of touch and ineffective in its witness to the world.

## Let the Light Shine

In his autobiography *Dear Me* the famous actor and raconteur Sir Peter Ustinov, tells of an occasion when he was holidaying on a friend's yacht in the Aegean. Suddenly, dense sea fog blanketed them, obliterating everything. Knowing they were somewhere near a Greek island famous for its scores of churches, the skipper vented his frustration by exclaiming, "So many churches, and so little light!" They're words that have a challenging resonance for us.

The fogs of moral and spiritual confusion have obliterated many of the landmarks that gave direction to earlier generations. Particularly from the 1960s, the prevailing winds of cynical secular humanism and godless materialism have blown a sandstorm of moral blindness into the eyes of modern people. And the tragedy is – the lightgivers are not operating!

While we give thanks for the many churches and organisations that do spread the light of the Gospel, it has to be said that far too often the church is failing to fulfil the role Jesus assigned her (Matthew 5:14-16).

In a vivid passage (Philippians 2:14-16) the Apostle Paul described the church as a constellation shining in the darkness of a *"crooked and depraved generation"*, giving bearings of moral and spiritual certainty to people who have lost their way.

So, why "so little light from so many churches"? One reason is that most people who claim to be Christians don't live biblically. Jesus described the light as *"your good works"* – behaviour that glorifies God. Paul described it as the distinctive quality of life seen in those who *"hold fast the word of life"* (NKJV) – that is, who allow the Word of God to shape their lifestyle as well as their doctrines. With its watering down of biblical standards in order to be politically correct, the church no longer offers clear moral guidance, and far too often the lifestyle of many Christians seems to be little different from the materialist pagans among whom they live.

In the NIV, Paul's words in Philippians 2:16 are translated differently – *"as you hold out the word of life"* – giving them a powerful evangelistic thrust which is so often missing in the church at large today. The lampshades of so-called religious tolerance have all but extinguished the claims of Christ to be "the only way". What Paul called *"the offence of the cross"* has caused many to switch off the evangelistic lights, or at any rate to diffuse them. Too many churches have lost a passion for the lost, and too many Christians are merely absorbed in themselves.

In many cases there is little light because so many modern churches and individual believers have simply run out of oil! (Matthew 25:1-13) The generators of the Spirit have almost seized through sheer neglect. The Spirit has been relegated to the back seat.

Betty Blaithwaite was keeper of the Walsey lighthouse, off Barrow in Furness, when one night the power supply failed. From 11pm to 3am she cranked the heavy machinery by hand until power was restored. "What sort of a lighthouse keeper would you be," she explained, "if you didn't care when your light failed? It's the whole driving point of the job!"

The Apostle Paul's challenge to the church of his day in Philippians 2:15, 16 needs to be faced afresh by us. In the words of *The Message* paraphrase: *"Go out into the world uncorrupted, a breath of fresh air in this squalid and polluted society. Provide people with a glimpse of good living and of the living God. Carry the light-giving Message into the night..."* Lord, help us to do it!

# *And Last of All!*

## *Are You a Spirit-filled "Pentecostal"?*

If you think that the headline poses a rather bizarre question, take another look at Acts 6:3. The early church was the finest example of what a truly "Pentecostal" church is like.

It was a church which had experienced the double outpourings of the Spirit recorded in Acts 2 and 4, and was a vibrant community living in the afterglow of those glorious events; yet when it came to the appointment of a "financial board", to handle a dispute over the "widows benevolent fund" the specifications are surprising: *"Pick out from among you seven men of good repute, full of the Spirit"* (ESV). The NIV is even more emphatic: *"Seven men who are known to be full of the Spirit."*

Why stipulate that? Surely they were all filled with the Spirit, weren't they? After all, they all belonged to that Spirit-blessed church, didn't they? Or, is it actually possible to belong to a Pentecostal or Charismatic church, to carry a Pentecostal ID card and not be truly Spirit-filled?

Looking more closely at the way the New Testament talks about being filled with the Spirit, it becomes clear that this means much more than being present at some outstanding spiritual event and being able to say "I was there when it happened", or even of having a personal experience of "receiving" the Spirit, whether in the "evangelical" sense of being born again or in the Pentecostal/ Charismatic sense of some initial infilling of the Spirit. In the New Testament sense, being filled with the Spirit is not an event but an ongoing experience. The question is not *"have you received the baptism in the Spirit?"* but *"are you continually being filled with the Spirit?"* So when Paul tells the Ephesians (5:17) *"to be filled with the Spirit"* he is using the continuous present tense of the verb, he is urging them to maintain something for which they are personally responsible.

In commenting on that verse, Dr Martyn Lloyd Jones points out that Paul, in his reference to the "alcohol culture" of the day, is drawing a comparison between the behaviour of the man in the world and the Christian. The worldly man goes to his tavern and gets drunk, and that has a profound effect on his behaviour, it results in "excess". He becomes "under the influence" of alcohol and says ridiculous things, sings bawdy songs and loses self control, as the pathetic results of binge drinking shown on TV news illustrate dramatically. In contrast, the Christian drinks deeply of the things of the Spirit and comes "under the influence" of the "new wine" of the kingdom (Matthew 9:17). That, too, has a profound effect upon him, on what he says and sings (Ephesians 5:19,20) and how he and his wife behave as partners and parents (Ephesians 5:21f). Far from losing self control, under the stimulus of the Spirit they acquire a new dignity and spiritual poise (Galatians 5:22,23). The important point, however, is that, in both cases, you have to drink! You cannot get drunk unless you drink heavily, you cannot be filled with the Spirit unless you come regularly to God's "bar" and actually open yourself up to all he offers – astonishingly, *"to the measure of all the fullness of God"* (Ephesians 3:19 NIV).

Life in the Spirit then is not an automatic condition which is switched on at conversion or by some initial spiritual experience; it is only maintained by careful and responsible attention to detail. Thus in Galatians 5:16-25 we are urged to live in the environment of the Spirit, to seek to be led by the Spirit, to open ourselves to the fruit-producing life of the Spirit, and to *"keep in step with the Spirit"*. In Ephesians 6:18 and Jude 20 we are told we must *"pray in the Spirit"* (cf Romans 8:26,27); in Philippians 3:3 and John 4:23,24 we are told that only those who worship in the Spirit are acceptable to God. In Romans 8:13 we are urged to deal with inner conflicts in the power of the Spirit; in 1 Corinthians 2:1-3 Paul reminds us that it is not clever communication skills but the power of the Spirit that makes ministry effective. Those three definitive words, *"in the Spirit"* are the key to authentic life and ministry. The truth is that we can quite easily operate outside those parameters. We can live, pray, worship, minister, do most things in the "flesh" – and we often do! When training, experiencing, know how and personal gifting kick in we may seem to be successful so far as human standards are concerned, but from God's perspective we may no longer be moving *"in the Spirit"* (see Galatians 3:3). It is uncomfortable to realise that we can be pastors, elders, worship leaders, musicians, administrators, youth leaders and a host of other things in a Pentecostal church and yet not be truly living under the anointing of Holy Spirit.

Living in the Spirit does not happen automatically; it only occurs when individual believers recognise their absolute dependence on the Spirit and consciously seek his enabling on a day-to-day basis. As Paul puts it in Romans 8:4-11, it means having *"the mind set on what the Spirit desires",* and through that "mindset" actually surrendering to the control of the Holy Spirit. It is a vibrant life focused on and absorbed with the things of the Spirit. Praying in the Spirit is not simply a matter of praying in tongues, valuable and inspiring though that is, it is a matter of seeking to understand the mind of the Spirit, responding to what he says through his Word and inner promptings, and seeking his energising power in prayer. Worship is not just a matter of singing the latest songs or getting the rhythm right; it is a matter of knowing the direction and the anointing of the Spirit. It is the same for every form of ministry and every aspect of personal life.

The truth is that we are only truly Spirit-filled when day by day we consciously recognise our need of his presence and power, when we do not rely upon past experience, knowledge of the Scriptures, our developed spiritual skills, or anything else, but when humbly we come before the throne of grace and seek for a fresh anointing.

One of my most precious memories is of a moment in a conference many years ago. In those days the members of the conference were mainly men; consequently the singing resembled a very large male voice choir. On this particular occasion we sang a hymn composed by

E.C.W Boulton, one of Elim's founding fathers, a verse of which seemed to be specially appropriate,

> *Under the anointing daily let me live,*
> *A priest and king;*
> *Relying not on human energy*
> *Thy smile to win.*
> *A simple soul in contact with my Lord,*
> *In whom all fullness is forever stored.*

To hear the deep harmony of a great assembly of pastors and leaders earnestly singing those words to the tune *Sandon* (*Lead Kindly Light*) was a moving moment that still resonates in my memory. It seemed to express what life and ministry are all about – "simple souls", without pretence, humbly and unaffectedly serving God, not trusting to human skills, but seeking the daily anointing of the Spirit.

The Lord Jesus himself said, *"without me you can do nothing"* (John 15:5), but he also promised to send *"another Helper"* to take his place and continue to be to the church all that he himself had been to his disciples (John 14:16,17,26; 16:13-15). The truth is that, without the Spirit we also can do nothing; yet so often we seem to ignore him and rely on our "human energy". Afresh we need to pray:

> "Lord, I cannot think, pray, worship, act or be what I should be today unless you fill me afresh with your Holy Spirit. Lord, I need you today. Let me live under the anointing of the Spirit. Please forgive my tendency to do my own thing without reference to you. Help me not resist or grieve or quench the Holy Spirit, but help me meet the challenges, take the opportunities, and live for your glory in all that I am and do today. Come, Holy Spirit, I need you! I ask this in the name and for the sake of the Lord Jesus. Amen."

And finally, it is possible to live like that because Jesus has said, *"If you... know how to give good gifts to your children, how much more will your Father give the Holy Spirit to those who ask him"* (Luke 11:13).